THE HARROWING OF HELL

An Epic Poem

J.S. Jackson

Illustrated by
Anastasiya Chybireva-Fender

"The Harrowing of Hell"
www.JonathanJackson.com
Copyright © 2010 by Jonathan Stevens Jackson
(TXu001721966 / 2010-10-08)
Copyright © 2021 by Jonathan Stevens Jackson
All rights reserved.

This book or parts thereof may not be reproduced in any form,
stored in a retrieval system, or transmitted in any form by any means
—electronic, mechanical, photocopy, recording, or otherwise—
without prior written permission of the publisher, except
as provided by United States of America copyright law.

Published by Hilasterion Publishing
5016 Spedale Court, # 234
Spring Hill, TN 37174

Printed in the United States of America

With special thanks to Mandi Hart and Mark Rodgers of
MORE Productions, and the Fathers of the Holy Mountain

For my three beautiful children,
who carry the mystery of God in their hearts.

The heart of Christianity is a myth, which is also a fact.
The old myth of the Dying God, without ceasing to be
myth, comes down from the heaven of legend
and imagination to the earth of history.[i]

C.S. Lewis

O proud, proud world!
Hast thou forgotten thy frailty?
Whence thy soul was lifted up,
Thy meekness melted into fanciful-snow,
Blown by temporal winds.

O lost, lost world!
Hast thou forgotten thy ballad?
Whence thy heart was purged of love,
Thy head absorbed delusional-diadems,
Wrought by evil's envy.

O sad, sad world!
Hast thou treaded beyond thy hearth?
Whence thy mind was draped in mire,
Thy eyes beckoned anomalous shades of woe,
Blackening the empyrean.

*For Christ also suffered once for sins,
the righteous for the unrighteous, that
he might bring us to God, being put to death
in the flesh but made alive in the spirit,
in which he went and proclaimed
to the spirits in prison,*

I Peter 3:18-19

PROLOGUE

All the spirits of Hell had assembled to witness the unparalleled proceedings, which were about to take place: generals and imps, wraiths and fiends alike, from the highest to the lowest order of the Underworld. They had all descended into the Sweltering-Hall of the deepest chasm of the Abode of the Dead, at the bequest of their Dark-Sovereign.

This was a region so loathsome and depraved, so vile and bleak that many of the lower-devils had never even dared to approach its burning-entrance. Each of them, at customary intervals, had joined in the trance-like revelry held in the Feasting Hall, to dine on the sins and souls of the dead—but this lair of darkness was reserved for a wholly other kind of banquet.

This was a momentous occasion unlike anything the cursed minds of evil had ever yearned for or dreamt or imagined.

They were all gathered around in a vast spiraling region, peering down, over an empty blasphemous-altar in the middle of the hall. The banished-spirits of Hell were salivating and panting almost uncontrollably. They were violently stomping their feet and pounding their weapons on the ground, releasing thunderous blasts of commotion and uproar. Their eyes were wide with insanity and rage, shifting colors and course with lawless rapidity and open pandemonium.

The Prince of Darkness slowly emerged out of the shadow-horde, which was parting like the infamous Red Sea to make a path for him—in envious-imitation of the Divine Power. He was a fierce and terrifying figure to behold: dark-red, black and purple reflections, with the most unnatural beauty and strength. He wore faint golden streaks on his head, which rested between his distorted-horns, and donned an enigmatic array of faded-armor. His eyes were black and utterly bereft of light. The Keys of Death and Hades hung heavy around his neck.

He seemed to release intonations of fear and power without speaking a word. The cadence of his dark eyes inflicted the entire atmosphere with the wound of intimidation and dread. He approached the jagged-altar. Satan was trembling within, but maintained an unassailable air of authority for the sake of his subordinates. The noise was deafening as he raised his right arm to silence them. In his

Prologue

hand, he held a wretchedly ominous sword-of-fire.

Within seconds, the Deepest Realm of Hell was unvoiced.

Then, the Father of Lies spoke:

"At this very hour! In the Middle-Sphere, Jesus the Nazarene is CRUCIFIED!!!" His voice echoed throughout the darkness and the multitude roared with furious delight. "Soon, we will receive Him and welcome Him into the realm of the dead!!!" Again, the manic-horde reverberated with elation.

"HADES!!!" he roared, "Prepare yourself!!! For this man feared death like any mortal and yet He claimed to be the Son of God!!! Prepare yourself for the FEAST OF FEASTS!!!!" The Sweltering-Hall began to shake and tremble from the pounding and roaring of the fiendish assembly.

Then, from the depths of the Underworld, like a great monster of the sea, the voice of Hades spoke above the revelry:

"Who is this JESUS you speak of?" The Great Hall was quickly silenced with fear, at the sound of Hades' thunderous voice. *"Thou hast told me that a mortal bearing this name hath taken away dead men from me; one called Lazarus among them..."*[ii]

A sense of dread began to fill the entire region. Satan, replied on behalf of the horde with calm authority. "It is the same man."

"BRING HIM NOT UNTO ME!" Hades bellowed back; his words hanging over the horde like a cloud of fear.

Lucifer, raised his voice forcefully, "Why are you afraid of this man Who Himself feared death!? In His life was He not our enemy!? And now, we have prevailed over Him! Am I not the Prince of the Underworld!?" Satan's voice swelled with rage and madness, "You will receive Him!!! And we will feast in our hour of Triumph!!!"

A dreadful-silence reigned in the Sweltering-Hall, which the accursed-spirits of hell could scarcely endure.

Finally, Hades spoke:

"As you desire, O Prince."

At once, the foundations of Hades trembled and quaked—a furious and violent wind blew through the Sweltering-Hall, causing panic throughout the realm. The windstorm slowly departed, leaving the demonic-horde restless and uneasy.

Lucifer's eyes slowly shifted towards the jagged- altar. "Wicked spirits of the Underworld, Depraved Devils of Anguish, behold the NAZARENE!!!"

The Ruler of Hell violently plunged his sword into the

heart of the altar with a horrifying scream! At the same moment, the wretched-weapon took on the shape of a burning-cross. The Sweltering-Hall erupted in feverish ecstasy, regaining their confidence.

Suddenly, a shadowy vision of Golgotha began to form above the altar, seamlessly melding with the diabolical-sword. Slowly, the bruised and mangled body of Jesus Christ of Nazareth, the Son of God, appeared before them—suspended upon the Cross—all but lifeless. His arms were spread out wide; the puncture wounds on His wrists and feet were open and fresh. A multitude of lashes were engraved on His defenseless skin, as crimson-liquid continued to pour out of Him. His face was marred and swollen, torn and frayed. A mixture of blood and sweat dripped from His forehead, where a scornful crown of thorns had deeply penetrated His earthen-brow, in unhallowed mockery.

The Prince of Hell continued with labored intentionality, not wanting to waste the moment: "I give you…" he raised both of his arms, stretching them out as far and as wide as they could reach; simultaneously the most magnificent, fearsome and imposing wings unveiled themselves before the crowd, amplifying the magnitude of his following words, "…the triumph of Death and Hades!!!"

The words resounded in warped echoes as the horde stood silently, transfixed by the coming manifestation.

The Patriarch of the Damned stood before the flaccid figure of Christ, almost unable to move, with the flames of Gehenna dancing behind him. After a few moments of euphoric silence, the Father of Lies spoke:

"His mortal life is ending in utter disgrace and despair—on a Roman Cross, no less! His followers have abandoned him and His own people did not receive Him. But, this is only the beginning of our triumph and revenge. Once He is here, with us—in the lowest realm of Hell—the real terror begins!"

More deafening shouts and cheers from the demonic throng ensued. The Prince of the Air continued over the ravenous and blistering noise, building upon their seditious lust and iniquitous chants, like a skilled conductor.

His movements were flawless and calculated, "He hangs powerless before us—as if His affliction were almost over—but there is another torment awaiting this 'Son of the Most High!' Look! Listen! His breathing is labored... wait... just wait..." Lucifer spun around, eyeing the entire space, as if to will the complete attention of every demon present. The Hall was once again silenced, but for the low rumbling of the surrounding flames.

Prologue

The Messiah began to tremble, releasing a cry of holy-defiance unlike anything the world or the underworld had ever heard; from the Cross, the Eternal Lamb of God cried out with a loud voice, "Eli, Eli, lama sabachthani?!"

Satan's black eyes piercingly burrowed into the cosmic-apparition from the Middle-Sphere. The shameful voice of the Fallen-Archangel continued to tremble as he spoke: "You are forever separated from the Father of Lights! Banished and condemned for all eternity! You belong to no one, are seen by no one and loved by no one! You are shut out and expelled from the Kingdom of Heaven—lost and abandoned to the agony of my will! You did not save them, son of Joseph! You did not save a single soul; they belong to me, now! All of them! You are nothing, You are a curse and a fraud; and You will never, never see or feel the light of love again! Cursed are You, false prophet! Cursed are You, son of perdition! You are a mortal corpse of corruption and darkness! You have been delivered over to the judgment-of-the-damned!!!"

The crowd erupted, the walls of Hell shook around them as if something cosmic and interminable were taking place, and indeed it was. The Enemy of Love was snuffing out the Light of the World like a defenseless candle, rendering the full force of condemnation.

The Son of God lifted His head and with all the strength left in His mortal body, whispered, "Father, into thy hands, I commit my spirit!" Suddenly, His form collapsed in a dead heap. The crowd continued to roar and bellow and howl their satisfaction and approval. Over the tumultuous absorption and delight, Lucifer screamed the three words he had most longed to voice since the inception of his rebellion, "GOD IS DEAD!!!"

And then in a flash, the mystical image of Golgotha was gone. Only the scorching-sword of damnation remained on the altar.

The sound gradually began to evaporate; the demonic mass was hushed with alarm. The Evil One stood erect, looking stunned and bewildered. He had not known what to expect after the execution had taken place. Would the soul of the Nazarene be delivered unto Hades immediately? Should He not appear on the blasphemous altar? Without allowing for another moment of uncertainty, the Author of Chaos quickly interjected, "Do not be troubled by this, slaves-of-hell; I have killed God's Son—and in so doing, I have killed man!" The blistering multitude received the words of their master with subordinate confidence; he retrieved his weapon and continued: "Fiends of Darkness and Spirits of Despair, in this very hour, in this very hall, I have triumphed over the Oppressor! I have overpowered the Most High! I have destroyed the Christ of God! He is *gone*! He is *dead*! Rest assured! He will be delivered to us soon enough! Everyone, to the Feasting Hall at once; we shall all drink and become intoxicated with the souls of the dead!"

The whole host began to disperse, with unbridled ecstasy quickly returning.

The Prince of Demons slowly began to walk away, but turned back one last time at the altar where the vision of Golgotha had occurred only moments before. He spoke under his breath: "Now, there is truly no hope for man."

I

INTO the darkness the Wounded-Light descended; the Immortal-Heart of Heaven, traversed deeper and deeper into the realm of the Absent-Light. His hallowed hands were still raw from the rust and steel His fallen Image-Bearers had viciously wielded against Him.

The glorious and ever-radiant Victor of Heaven walked through the blackness of the earthen walls—His ghostly feet, aching from the punctured nail-wounds inflicted upon the Middle-Sphere—His brow was swollen and tender from the mocking thorns, which had been cruelly pressed into His sacred flesh on the fateful mountain called The Skull.

The Lord of flesh and spirit moved speedily, through the rancid mud and glowing flames; with each step, His mortal-robe was rapidly healing itself, transforming into the armor of immortality. The Everlasting Flame, Who had spoken the worlds into existence through a shared vision of harmonious bliss and simple utterance of what *was*, began to breathe with imperishable lungs. His scarlet bloodstream was now flowing with more force than the oceans of the earth. But, the Light of the World was still wrapt in darkness, for His eyes could see only the shadows of the flames.

The Lion of Heaven stopped suddenly, His oracle-lungs burning from the poisoned air of solitude and want. He, who had healed the blind, could see only shadows. He, who had fashioned the celestial choirs with voice and song, could hear only silence and the rhythm of His own breathing. The Maker of Eyes stared into the blackness, as if to somehow bend it to His Sovereign will. The darkness obeyed Him.

The shadows began to scurry and flee like the sounder of swine, which ran into the raging mouth of the sea, during His earthly life. It was still dim, but the Master of the Elements could now perceive beyond a mere dream-like instinct, where He was and where His steps were leading Him.

Beyond the walls, the Sea-Calmer began to hear the faintest sounds of wailing souls. The desperate voices rose within His unblemished mind like smoke before a sacred temple. Then, behind the wailing voices, He began to hear most clearly, the vile, malignant cheers and boasts of demons. "The Lord is dead! The Lord is dead! Crucified, how sweet! The Lord is dead! The Lord is dead! Make haste to the feast! Make haste!" The bloodthirsty chants continued to rage and fuse with the screams and cries of Adam's Children—a most horrifying demonic symphony of corrupted jubilance.

The Savior's stomach turned within Him and His eyes began to moisten. He reached out His hand and began to burn an ancient utterance into the walls of Hell, '*I have led captivity captive.*' The burning hand of the Almighty slowly fell to His waist side. Behind the fiery words the shape of a door mystically appeared. The Son of Paradise blinked in astonishment; the Souls of the Righteous were on the other side! With the passion-of-heaven, the Son of God lifted His right arm to enter the unknown realm; but the faintest whisper arose within, *"Find the Patriarch. You must find the Patriarch."* The Healer of Humanity removed His hand in obedience and the cryptic-door faded from sight; all that remained were the words He had burned into the walls of perdition.

The Virgin's Son gracefully raised His eyes toward the winding caverns before Him. The Christ of Nazareth longed to save every soul, but in wisdom, He knew that many would not come with Him, because their hearts were poisoned with the wine of delusion and the mead of pride; conceit was their god and master, the fountain in which they bathed.

Suddenly, the feet, which trodden the bloody path to Calvary moved beneath Him. The walls were narrow and the caverns were short and various. Each seemed to end only seconds after they had begun, blurring His surroundings like a whirling vision. Torches lined the sharp and jagged walls and the Shepherd of Souls was constantly being thrown in and out of darkness—but His revelatory countenance was fixed and strong.

The voices grew nearer, the heat increased, and the heart within the Wisdom of Heaven beat faster and faster. Lower and lower, the King of Angels descended into the pit of corruption.

In the distance, the Everlasting Warrior, Who had suffered death for all, saw the shape of three demons, He knew them all by name; what they used to look like before the war in heaven, what their fate could have been, had they chosen to remain true to the light.

"Balsius, Draylon, Fiendeo!" The three demons turned in absolute fear at the sound of His voice and immediately fell to their knees, shaking. The Son of The Most High peered down and with only a thought, bound them to their place. "Balsius…" the Lord spoke; the ancient demon was trembling uncontrollably, "take Me to the Feasting Hall," He said in a terrifying whisper.

Balsius fearfully rose to his feet and began to walk down one of the cavernous hallways. The Lord of Light whispered to Himself in an unknown tongue, the demon Balsius continued to contort in agony with every sacred syllable. The chaotic revelry was coming closer and closer as the Prince of Peace broadened His shoulders, ready for the eternal moment.

Suddenly, the narrow, torch-lit cave opened up to a vast and burning gulf. Layer upon layer of descending dungeons and fiery caverns came into view. The sounds of demonic rapture and the bemoaning souls of men reverberated before the Ruler of Spirits and the King of Psalms.

The fallen-mutilated-angel shook quietly next to Him, "Go back to your cave, cursed one," The Light spoke with measured prudence. Balsius scurried away in tormented relief. The Champion of Realms walked into the heat of the Absent-Light and peered down, across the ravine, observing the plight of those who had chosen darkness over light, hatred over love, revenge over mercy, lust over fidelity and self over the Ancient of Days. Compassion rushed through His sacred-bloodstream, just below the surface of His transient-skin, protecting His phantom-frame like a holy shield.

Six levels below Him, across the great chasm, The Prince of Heaven could see Lucifer, the once-splendid, radiant

and magnificent Light-Bearer, seated on a flaming throne of decadence and murder. His appearance was powerful and gloriously adorned with innumerable corrupted attributes of The Most High. Satan was feasting on the souls of the dead, raising his dark, golden cup high into the air, toasting with his various miserable devils.

The eyes of Christ shifted to the myriad chambers around and below Him, of shackled souls; self-gods locked in the unseen shadows of their own loathing. Each one, He knew by name; the Spirit, Who was raising Him from the dead, imparted this knowledge upon every glance. He saw their creation, their longings, their fears and sins—He saw their hopes and He heard their prayers inside of His mind, since time immemorial. His eyes filled with tears, as He looked upon each of them.

Then, the Second Adam gracefully lifted His robe off and gently laid it on the burning ground beside Him. The Son of Man stood naked, overlooking the pit of utter corruption and hopelessness. As He did this, a dazzling celestial light began to emanate from His spirit-form.

The heads of demons from the lowest to the highest order began to turn at the alien-sight. The eyes of men and women, lost in the blindness of rage and remorse opened and began to stare; transfixed and almost wounded by the foreign vision.

The Evil One, himself, peered across the divide in abject horror, dropping his golden cup of triumph onto the ashes beneath him.

The revelry ceased. The wailing subsided, little by little until there was absolute silence in the halls of perdition. Every demon fell to his knees, trembling in terror. The spirit-bodies of Adam's children, fell prostrate in fearful reverence. Satan could not move; the authority of the Eternal One had bound all of his supernatural faculties.

Then, in the presence of the Hordes of Hell, before the throne of Satan and his assemblies, to the fallen beloved, The Mercy of Heaven spoke, His voice echoing over the darkness:

"The Eternal Lamb of God, was crucified—and is raised from the dead, in accordance with the imperishable Word-of-the-Almighty! I, the Everlasting Lamb of God, have taken away the sins of the world! I, the Lion of the Tribe of Judah have devoured the lies of your ruler! I, even I, the Alpha and the Omega, the Beginning and the End, have reconciled the sons of Adam and the Daughters of Eve to My Heavenly Father! This fallen and cursed angel that you serve..." the Apocalyptic Prophet pointed directly at Satan from across the divide, who was fuming, but still unable to speak, "...this Father of Lies and Ruler of Chaos, has no power over you any longer! Look with your eyes and see how he has not the strength to speak or the will to fight! He is powerless against My Gospel of Grace! Come pagans! Come heathens! Come barbarians and brutes! Come sinners and fallen ones! All who yearned for Me in blindness, come and see with your own eyes the consummation of your desire and the fulfillment of your ignorant faith! Those who worshipped myths and legends, bowing before idols of superstition and stone, come and receive the blessed wine of Truth and Redemption! Come sons of mercy! Come daughters of grace! I AM the Salvation of your soul! Come drunkards, swindlers and thieves! Come wayward children of My Father and inherit the kingdom, which has been prepared for you from the foundation of the world! Cast off the shackles of wickedness and despair; receive the wisdom of the Father of Lights! Abandon yourselves and run into the Land of the Living! All sins have been forgiven! I have overcome the world! I have led captivity captive! I have crushed the serpent's head! I have swallowed up death! Come and drink! Come to the heavenly banquet! I offer you My Body and My Blood as your amnesty and incorruptible joy! This, is your immortal-hour of redemption!"

    Silence hung over the deep; dancing flames whispered

to one another without apprehension, mimicking the curse of Babel. Every soul beheld the Man. The Bright and Morning Star clothed Himself again with the humble robe of a Nazarene. The Legions of Tophet and Fiends of Gehenna were silent, enveloped in the terror, which only fallen angels possess the knowledge of.

The Cross-Bearer looked down, beyond the Feasting Hall to the east of Him, spotting the River of Acheron flowing and burning with anguish. He looked again at the Enemy of Love, who was seething upon his wretched throne. The Word of God raised His mighty right hand and gently touched His lips, releasing the Serpent from his silence; even upon this hour, the Master of Heaven would not violate the freedom of man to choose his eternal-fate.

Satan let out a roar more thunderous than any the earth, or her creatures, had ever heard. The hordes of demons awoke from their trance, repositioning themselves for defense. The Ruler of Hell called for his scepter and began to advance to another post. One of his generals, who was still standing in shock, spoke, "What shall we do now, master?" Satan turned around inflamed, "What we always do… LIE!!!"

His face trembled with madness and rage. The demon responded, "But what do we do about…" the fiend could not bear to speak the Lord's Name, "…about Him?" he whispered. Satan thundered back, "He won't force the humans to believe. It doesn't matter what the truth is. It matters what they believe! Listen to your father, all of us were unjustly banished from the Celestial Realm, and now, we will banish the Nazarene from our kingdom. We will spew the most glorious venom the Underworld has ever seen and send this feeble Christ back to His oppressive Father with despair and turmoil over the vanity of His crucifixion!"

The demonic horde regained an inkling of maniacal confidence and began to march into the dense shadowy-halls, following their Deplorable Ruler.

The Christ of Paradise moved quickly; time was not alive in this realm in the mortal-sense; but urgency was. He was to take His Gospel to all the aching souls of abandoned faith—one by one, in mystical glory. He was to speak below the incessant din of distortion and lies, touching the space of holiness bound within the lost and wayward descendants of Adam. He was to look them in the eye, and offer the miracle of reconciliation and boundless-grace. He carried within Him the weight of His Eternal Father's intention; all was to be accomplished, before the rising of the earth-sun on the third day of the transient-age.

II

THE wailing-voices of men and women were now circling the atmosphere in closer proximity. Many were crying out for the Savior to come to them, but most were screaming with vile displays of anger and indignation. Innumerable demons scurried out of His path as He made His way down toward the chamber-of-souls. The dark path was winding and disorienting to the natural senses. The pit seemed endless, a hopeless abyss of utter grief and isolation.

The Wave-Walker traversed upon the fiery ground, leaving sacred footprints in His wake, which the very flames of Hell could not demolish. He reached the first chamber. A trembling figure appeared to Him in the corner of the cell, lying in a fetal position. The entrance was barred with flaming curses that swirled and morphed seamlessly before Him. Jesus reached out His hand and touched the scorching-barrier, disintegrating the mirage. He stepped inside. The figure was cursing incessantly, clawing and scratching itself in condemnation. The ghost was facing the empty, black wall and its disheveled long hair was covering its face. It was as if this living-thing had always been there and also as if it had only just arrived; for this realm was outside the epoch of temporal-dimensions.

The Author of Wombs knelt down before the shaking soul and placed His hand on its shoulder: "Absalom," His voice rang out. The figure jolted to his knees in absolute fear, gazing wildly into the Eyes of Grace. "Precious Absalom, I have come to bring you home; to your Heavenly Father, and to your earthly father, David. He waits for you; even now he is praying for you. I know you heard Me, when I spoke from the Upper-Height—surely, you heard the voice of the Forerunner, echoing throughout these halls, when he prophesied of My descent into this realm. Was not every soul forewarned? Did you not believe that this would indeed, take place? I have come for you—I have paid for your sins, Absalom; each and every one of them—even the betrayal of your father. Come with Me. No shame awaits you, only grace and mercy. The moment has come, child of Abraham. Receive Me, and you have received life-eternal."

The figure, which shook before Him, appeared almost inhuman. This son-of-Israel's-king looked as much like a beast as a man. The sacred dignity of bearing the Image was so dimmed and subdued that he seemed only one breath away from utter barbarism; a dreadful scapegrace. Still, the Lord of War was before him and hope had never drawn so near. The faded creature caught eyes with the Christ.

Suddenly, a demon appeared from the deepest recess of the cave. A small, hunched over, black-and-scarlet-wraith moved closer to the suffering Absalom. The wraith wore a chain around its ankle, which was fastened tightly to the human. The evil spirit cautiously positioned itself by the left ear of the man, avoiding all eye contact with the Lord of Redemption and spoke:

"If what this madman says is true, then why are you still in chains, betrayer? Why, if your sins have been atoned for, as He says, are you still bathing in the fire of your own lust for power? This Man is a charlatan, a hopeless, naïve dreamer. You were sent here for a reason, and don't you forget that; many, many reasons. You were born a curse on the House of David. You are a disgrace to your father's crown. You have always been unworthy to inherit the blessings of the righteous. Is God unjust? Would He allow a wretched, deceitful stain like you to inherit life in the Upper-Realm? Never. I tell you this, human-stain, what this errant-prophet calls Heaven, would be for you, absolute Hell. How could you show yourself in that Realm?

How could you face your father? All would know of the grave sins, which you have committed. You would be forced to live in the fierce, unsheltered light of shame and everlasting-disgrace. At least here, all are ignorant of your existence. At least here, the only shame you feel is from yourself. Imagine; imagine the *weight* of those saintly bystanders, gazing at you in horror. Imagine the disgust and rightly so, rightly so. No, wretched creature—you are what you are and this flawed Carpenter knows nothing of your true wickedness; if He did, He most assuredly would have never stopped to speak with you. A wretched soul is what you are, a wretched soul."

    The fiend let the silence hang in the mind of Absalom like a tolling bell, quite proud of his hellish-aria. He leaned over and began to write in the scorching-sand; it was a doleful-poem that Absalom's father had written on the day of his son's betrayal. The demon leisurely whispered the words as he transcribed them. "Hear the words of your father:

In this hour, I have born the curse of this crown
It holds no strength to sway, save a mournful sound
I am not a king beneath this mantle-glow
But a weeping father, whose heart is shadowed,
By the memory of a boy I have loved,
Since birth,
Of all the foes I've faced from giants to beasts,
None have summoned such fear in my waking soul,
As the account of my beloved, deceased.
Rather would a lion have devoured me,
Or the blunt-sword of Goliath impaled me,
Straight through,

Than the agony of this cup of sorrow,
For it is bile in my mouth; a monstrous-plague;
To watch the river of familial-waters,
Turn into a poisoned-pool of crimson blood,
The ending-of-the-dawn is upon my spirit,
This night,

I shall never cease to rue my son's deceit

The Lamb of God broke the devious trance-of-shame with the majesty of His voice: "Absalom, look at Me; you are not evil unless you choose to remain so. All you have to do is take My hand and the chains shall be loosed. Your sins are forgiven, precious Absalom. There is no other way, for any man to enter My kingdom; even your father. Remember his words, 'Have mercy on me O God, according to Your steadfast love; according to Your abundant mercy blot out my transgressions. Wash me thoroughly from my iniquity, and cleanse me from my sin!' *Mercy* Absalom, not sacrifice, is the way to heaven. I AM your Righteousness, son. I AM your sacrifice. I AM your perfection. Salvation is yours by blood, if you choose to receive Me. Take My hand, now, and follow Me."

The Servant of God reached out His nail-scarred hand, passionately awaiting the ultimate choice.

Absalom was writhing in torment, fighting the internal pull of darkness. He could not speak to the Ruler of Heaven, but his eyes were locked on the Anointed One, peering far into the endless ocean of mercy. Then, astonishingly, the lost son of David reached out his withering hand and touched the Messiah's. Immediately, the phantom-chains broke and fell lifeless on the ground. The vile demon shrieked and hid in the shadows, fearing the coming judgment.

The One Who raised Lazarus from the dead pulled the faded creature up to his feet and lightly brushed his hair from his face; Absalom's countenance was already beginning to change. The smallest glimpse of the Image was returning to him. "Come with Me, we've much to do before we ascend," the Warrior of Heaven spoke as He stepped out of the cave onto the blazing ledge of damnation.

The next-chamber was only a few steps away and the Architect of Miracles entered quickly. Absalom followed behind, in complete awe; mesmerized at the sight of the Lord. A young woman, by earthly-appearances, stood erect, chained to a burning wall, swaying back and forth in emotional agony. When the woman caught sight of the Walking-Light, her eyes went blind and she fell to her knees weeping, crying out for salvation.

Six spirits of corruption emerged from the gloomy shadows, side by side, forming a demonic wall of resistance between the woman and the Lord, in vain hope that their perverse-solidarity would challenge the authority of the Most High. Shiloh said nothing, but simply lifted His sacred hand, exposing His pierced palm: a brilliant beam-of-light flew out from His wounded palm—the pure force of it destroyed the wall-of-demons instantly. The woman wept with her face buried in her hands, in shame.

Her voice was filled with distressful inarticulate sounds of regret and trauma. Jesus quickly knelt down beside her and whispered in her ear.

The trembling woman screamed without cognizance; it was the Scream-of-Exorcism. Four wicked spirits tore from her transient-skin and fled her ghostly-body, vanishing into the darkness. Absalom watched in silent amazement as Jesus touched her eyes, restoring her sight *and* her sanity. The young woman stared feebly at her Humble Savior. He whispered again in her ear; the faintest smile flashed across her worn face. She was indeed a beautiful creature: her name was Delilah.

Christ rose to His feet with His beloved Delilah and hastily walked out of the chamber.

The following moments were a blur-of-flashes; light colliding with darkness, shadows clashing with flames, furious chains unfettered and souls benighted no more. Within the wake of liberation, hundreds of souls began to follow the light in imitation of Heaven's Sun; every race, tribe, culture and tongue were seen and heard in the converging storm. It was almost as if this wake was a River of Light, parting the scorching seas of Hades. The Blood and Atonement of this Transcendent-Sacrifice had abolished the authority of Hell, once endowed to the Father of Lies

through Adam's original-transgression.

The Ruler of the Universe took ground furiously, unrestrained by the darkness. He was moving within a realm unknown to the natural world; He could profess and proclaim the full richness of the prophets and the Law within a moment of sporadic-light. He could reveal the complete-chronicle of a broken soul within one glance. The same Word, Who proclaimed over darkness, "Let there be light," and the world was—spoke in the tongues of heaven—within the mystery of the Eternal-Trinity-Dawn.

The Harrowing of Hell was consuming hordes of demons; the very composition of the Netherworld was transforming within minutes. Multitudes of fierce and stalwart devils were ascending and descending upon the Wake of Light, but the rays-of-redemption extinguished each deplorable-demon. Any soul, who found himself in the Savior's Wake, was protected from the rage and madness of these fearsome-beasts, with bloodthirsty fangs and enlarged eyes.

Satan had remained concealed, since he had vanished into the darkness of the nearest cavern. It was unknown whether his absence was brought upon by intolerable fear, or by some foul-strategy awaiting a meticulous moment.

Suddenly, the Lord of the Living came to a halt before a

certain prison. The River of Souls came to a silent, hastening cessation behind Him. The innumerable sounds of the Underworld continued to swirl above and around them. The Oracle-King stared fiercely at the shadow of a woman, lost behind a thick-darkness. He transgressed the dim threshold of the Abode of the Dead and approached the estranged-soul with the fire of heaven in His eyes.

The woman was faded, almost to the point of a devil. Her eyes were filled with madness and poison. As the Christ came nearer, she rose to her feet and positioned her spirit-form into a seductive display. Worms and maggots slithered and crawled in and out of her figure. She was drunk with murder and possessed with vanity.

The Christ of Compassion spoke—the woman alone could hear His hushed voice:

"I know your deeds, daughter of destruction; they are evil and they are many," her mouth opened in disgust, as if she were about to vomit, "But I took upon Myself, the condemnation that was due to you, Daughter of Eve—and even now, in the Abode of the Dead, I can be your Salvation, if you repent and receive the Spirit of God." The woman convulsed and screamed a most unnatural bellowing. Demons flew from her mouth like fire and worms began to multiply, departing from her wraith-like form. She looked at the Nazarene with venom and malevolence.

The Savior continued:

"Horses of justice ended your mortal life—and your name, *Jezebel*, is a curse upon the whole earth. But, I offer you a new name, a new heart and a new destiny. I will never turn you away. Make your choice, daughter of heaven." The ghost of perdition bellowed with the strength of a thousand demons, causing a whirlwind to invade the prison. The Judge of the Earth spoke with heavenly sorrow, "Even now… even now you are what you have chosen to be. You shall never see My face again."

And with that, the Mighty One, the God of Eden walked out of the whirlwind and departed.

The myriad-souls who were following the Light of the World began to grow in strength and number. Their appearance was also changing rapidly as they traversed upon the brazen-ground. Their skin and hair were seamlessly transforming into something, which the living might actually recognize and proclaim as—*human*.

Their original awareness and reasoning faculties were also returning to them in varying degrees of velocity and power. Many of them were shocked to discover luminous-weapons in their hands, which they had not possessed only moments before: swords, axes, bows and arrows, spears and shields—all engraved and constructed with the most unique designs of the highest realm of illumination.

A small army was forming.

But the patriarchs of perversion and deceit were not done waging their war—they were not willing to accept defeat, even in the face of such a bold display of authority by the Servant of God.

The nascent-army-of-heaven made its way into the lower depths of Hell. They moved quickly, swinging their swords, shooting their arrows and throwing their spears, impaling the minions of darkness left, right and overhead. It seemed as if there was no end to the onslaught of warfare.

The fearsome multitude-of-light were all speaking and whispering in a chorus of unknown tongues, without reserve. Souls were being grafted into the river and added to their number, every passing second. Each of them, men and women alike, felt the rush and adrenaline of wounding or destroying the very agents, which only moments before had held them in, what seemed to be, eternal-captivity.

Their eyes flashed with the vengeance of heaven. They descended lower and lower into the burning blackness. They battled through the spiraling second and third realms, grafting more and more repentant-offspring into the glow of revivification.

Most who followed Him, possessed little care as to His strategy or plan of attack. They simply wished to remain in the Wake of Light and to increase their strength and luminosity. But, after fighting through the winding fourth and fifth spheres of the Underworld, a small number of the Children-of-Illumination began to seek understanding in their hearts, as to the strategy of their Radiant Ruler. Where was He headed? What was His plan? But, they did not voice these questions.

His line of attack was unknown to every living thing, except the mysterious Logos of God, Himself.

III

THEY were now approaching the sixth-level of anguish, where the Feasting Hall was boastfully arrayed. They were traveling on the east side of the serpent's winding-habitation. Across the divide, one could see the throne where Lucifer had been seated, when the Son of Man had given His glorious appeal to the souls-imprisoned. The Feasting Hall was completely deserted now; abandoned in the chaos of the grace-invasion—except for the vestige of suffering souls, which were lying in bewilderment and pain, unable to move or escape, even though they were unguarded.

The Compassionate Ruler of the Ages slowed to a stop, as the cries and moans of the afflicted caught His attention.

There were fire-cells to His left, filled with men and women who were crying and reaching out to Him. The Creator of Spirits lifted His hand towards the blazing-curtain, which enslaved the various children of God. The Divine Light burned much hotter than the inferno-barrier; at once releasing the penitent-captives, allowing them to enter the

Wake of Light. He touched the eyes or the hands or the heart of each person who fled from the darkness—imparting symphonies and sonnets of intimate mysteries and secrets into every one of them. Each of them heard their name being spoken, even though the Master never opened His mouth; they were all being infused with divine revelation and consolation.

He continued His intricate actions of liberation with countless other cells, while the Newly-Redeemed fended off the assorted attacks of lesser-minions. For every assemblage of souls that ran to the Nazarene for rescue, there were almost as many who recoiled in fear and suspicion—not believing or trusting what they were witnessing.

They feared it was a trick or a mirage and doubted whether or not one could actually escape Hell. If they could not, and they had tried to escape, their punishment would only increase. Still, others were merely enraged; consumed with darkness and evil-intent. They screamed profanities—spitting and shrieking at the Son of God, as well as cursing the fleeing-fugitives, who were entering His shelter.

The Christ of Heaven promptly led the ragged army over a narrow-blackened-bridge into the middle-region of the Feasting Hall. The faded figures of men and women were strewn about the tables, chairs and floor, releasing a chorus of haunting agony.

Through the power of the Undiminished Spirit, the Christ perceived that many of these children were of Noah's generation. They had heard the prophetic declarations of the coming flood, but had mocked Noah and jeered him day and night. Some were speaking an array of unintelligible words; while others were crying out, as if they were reliving the earthly-judgment.

One of the men was screaming in delusional-panic: *"Open the doors!"* A woman was shouting at the top of her worn and pillaged lungs: *"Come back for us! Please come back!"* She was curled up in a fetal position, writhing in desperation.

Tears suddenly filled the eyes of the Divine Judge. He moved to his knees next to the woman and lifted her from the smoldering ground. She awoke from her nightmare and tried to regain focus, but was unable to perceive what was occurring. In truth, there was very little separation from her present state and her recurring nightmare.

She had brown skin, amber eyes and long flowing black hair. She stared at the Face of Forgiveness and slowly began to sense the impossible: someone from the Superior Realm had infiltrated the Abyss, to free *her*. And then, all at once, she suddenly knew Who it was that was holding her, even though she knew not His name.

He spoke quietly to her: "Beloved Soniah, I AM The Way out of this place—I AM the Door to the Ark, and I can save you from the rains of judgment and the torrent of condemnation. Will you follow Me, beloved?" She blinked the tears out of her amber eyes and nodded her head in euphoric-astonishment. He carefully set her down on her feet and handed her off to Absalom, who was still close behind Him.

Others began to stir from their nightmares and hallucinations. The Lion of Justice began to call their names out loud, summoning them to His side. Again, many staggered towards the Light, but others fled in fear. The River of Light widened as the sacred-warriors moved in supernatural symmetry, equipping each of the new renegades with multiple weapons and shields.

The Vanquisher of Death swept His hand over the atmosphere and the entire hall was blanketed with purifying light.

Absalom watched, dumbstruck by the display. The words of his father rushed into his mind: "Where shall I go from your Spirit? Or where shall I flee from your presence? If I ascend to heaven, you are there! If I make my bed in Sheol, you are there! If I take the wings of the morning and dwell in the uttermost parts of the sea, even there your hand shall lead me, and your right hand shall hold me. If I say, 'Surely the darkness shall cover me, and the light about me be night,' even the darkness is not dark to you; the night is bright as the day, for darkness is as light with you…"

It came over him like a wave: he had never been fully-separated from God, even in the pit of despair and the bed of Sheol. Somehow, God had been with him in his guilt and torment, keeping him alive for this hour-of-redemption. The revelation filled him with such resplendent awe that he nearly bent over and collapsed onto his knees from the sheer weight of it. But, the presence of the Refulgent River, as well as the raging battle that surrounded him, steadied his balance and kept him on his feet.

Absalom was gently holding on to Soniah's arm—a protective instinct to console her. At his feet he discovered a breastplate, fashioned with chain-mail and a gleaming metallic sword. He knew without hesitation that this belonged to the woman he was holding on to. He bent down and picked them up, offering them to her.

Soniah's eyes were wide, taking in every moment, barely remembering to breathe. She took the coat of mail and the sword, eyeing the inscription on it. It was in a language that was foreign to Absalom, but obviously known to her, for her eyes filled with tears upon reading it.

Others were gathering around them and the Wake was widening like a living organism. Archers continued to fend off the shadow-devils that leapt from unseen crevices above them and attacked from the numerous corners and caves of the sixth-level.

The Lord of War turned around and addressed His army: "The River of Acheron is just below us, on the seventh-region, flowing and burning with anguish and contempt for the Living God. You shall no doubt encounter its ancient water-beasts and sea-demons. They are vast and unmerciful."

His eyes narrowed with fearsome intent: "*Stay in the Shadow of My Light!* Do not be afraid, little ones, for you are mighty! Fight as one, speak to the darkness in My Name and you shall defeat it! Do not stray from the light!"

He raised His radiant right hand and waved for them to follow Him, once again. Their faces were a mixture of courage and intimidation. Some of the less-transparent figures were comforting and emboldening the more-faded souls. Everyone was at a differing pace of transformation and sought to either reassure or receive encouragement, depending on their current state of existence.

The Avenger of Heaven led them around the western wall of the sixth-level, freeing countless slaves and administering justice to the ungodly spirits that continuously crawled out of the corners, like swarms of maniacal cockroaches.

It seemed as if the Overseer of Souls, by descending further and further into the Abyss of Destruction, was intent on returning to the Sweltering-Hall of the Abode of the Dead: the very place where the Prince of Demons unleashed his torrent of condemnation on the Christ of Nazareth.

The humble Host of Heaven wrapped around the spiraling-passageway, descending into the eastern side of the seventh-level of Hades.

IV

Flowing fiercely and rushing with peril before them, was the River of Acheron. It was not made of natural water, but a kind of fire, that moved and breathed like water. The strange and powerful lava was bursting sporadically with scorching air pockets from underneath. The presence of unnatural-spirits could be felt but not yet seen. The temptation of fear blew over the Shepherd's army like a gust of unholy wind.

The Commander of Heaven spoke to His infantry: "Archers! Take high ground and ready your bows! All who carry spears, climb the jagged walls and take aim! Those who bear axes and swords; follow Me and fear not the ancient wrath of Hell, for the divine wrath of My Father is fiercer than any fallen creature or spirit! Take heart, children of the light and believe!!!"

The army cheered and began to position themselves as their Hallowed Guide had commanded. Suddenly, an enormous sea-beast broke the surface lunging for the nearest light-inhabitant, barely missing its prey. Some of the archers were able to release their arrows in time and, to their astonishment, they split into multiple arrows, changing directions with speed and intelligence, striking the sea-monster in several places as it fell back underneath the smoldering waves.

Another creature burst forth, twenty feet down the river, lunging itself onto the burning ground, releasing reptile-like legs for a quick pursuit. Its mouth was vicious and its eyes were filled with bloodlust. It was not alone, another of the same kind emerged behind it, looking just as lethal as its predecessor.

Those with spears began to throw them, joining in with archers above them. As they waged war from the air, the Blessed and Fearless Warrior stepped out onto the River of Acheron, without burning or sinking. His swordsmen and ax-bearers were stunned and baffled.

Hundreds of anaconda-like serpents began to slither out of the lake and attack the soldiers who were still on land. They fended them off as best they could, feeling overwhelmed and panicked. The Wave-Walker called to them from the fire: "Come to Me! Don't be afraid; step into the fire, it shall not burn you! You are clothed with righteousness! Come!"

Absalom was the first to bravely step onto the scorching river, discerning that there was soon to be no other sound choice—and to his amazement; he did not sink or burn. Other's quickly followed, evading the poisonous-teeth of the atrocious-sea-serpents.

The archers and the spear-warriors managed to slay the first monster with innumerous arrows and spears, but the second beast was still advancing. One of the spear-fighters leaped down, to strike the gruesome creature directly in the open mouth, but he was not fast enough and the beast lunged forward, sinking its teeth into the spear-man's shoulder, piercing through his armor and drawing blood.

The soldier stumbled back and fell as the other embattled men and women leapt down from their crevasses upon the merciless-beast, plunging their weapons into its physique; forcing it to collapse in defeat. The wounded combatant, crawled on his knees and leaned against the uneven wall in severe pain.

The Seer-Christ observed the growing threat all around them: the repulsively large serpents slithering onto the riverbank, the erratic-surfacing of the great sea-monsters; and now, He could see the formation of an aerial attack along the upper-ledges. He quickly retrieved an ageless sword from the inside of His robe and lifted it in the air as He spoke:

"Citizens of Heaven, attend to My instructions and heed My commands, and all of you shall live! Archers, look to the air above you and leave the water-beasts to the spear-holders! Swordsmen and Ax-carriers, slay as many serpents as you can and remain on the blazing-river until I return! Fight as one! The hope of Heaven is your strength! Do not give in to fear, even when you cannot see Me!"

And with those cryptic words the Radiance of God dove beneath the scorching waters and vanished from sight.

Below the surface, the Seed of Abraham descended through the dense fiery river with enormous speed and velocity. A brilliant mantle of luminosity covered Him, and He could see the ascending leviathans and sea-beasts ubiquitously, because of the light, which was emanating from Him. He was striking and slashing them left and right with the

fury of paradise and His eternal sword flashed upon every impact. His mane was flowing and His eyes were shimmering amidst the visible chaos.

One of the serpents had craftily managed to wrap itself around His waist, swirling quickly to bind His arms and render Him defenseless. But the Root of Jesse swung His sacred sword with all of His hallowed might and beheaded the creature before it could advance any further upon Him. He threw the slain-leviathan off and continued His epic incursion of the River of Acheron.

He knew His fragile army was waging war above the surface and the names of each redeemed-soul urged Him on with increasing intensity. As He flew through the dark-red and yellow sea, He leapt onto the stony-back of an appalling beast. The dreadful creature spun instinctively with great force to throw the Warrior-Prince off its back. The Elysian Knight held on and began to move toward the beast's stomach: its most vulnerable region.

He grabbed the stony scales along the monster's back and sides, allowing Him to maneuver swiftly underneath. The enraged beast was still spinning wildly as the Righteous Invader plunged His sword into its bowels, impaling the diabolical beast with one stalwart carving.

The Incarnate Word traversed deeper and deeper into the belly of Acheron, slaying every sea-demon He could reach. As He approached the bottom of the chasm He began to observe that every leviathan and deplorable-monster was originating from a singular source: a vast multifaceted, octopus-like Principality. It was releasing hundreds-of-thousands of creatures at once, from a host of diverse openings. At the center of the stronghold was the shape of six large iridescent-eyes, darting around in hellish orchestration.

The Valiant Ruler of Heaven escalated His pace and headed straight for the bosom of the pandemonium. His speed was blinding and His mantle-of-light, impenetrable. He readied His sword for the final collision. The watery-creatures were no longer attempting to constrain His beam of light, for it was too bright and fierce for their darkened dispositions to battle.

As the Hero of Men and Angels approached the ungodly temple of the burning river, all six eyes of the Principality turned and gazed upon their coming-doom.

The Son of Heaven burst through the remaining tentacles of the Nefarious Tiamat and struck it with the unparalleled force of Light! The entire sea began to tremble and shake as the monstrous structure writhed in pain, swaying back and forth.

The Eternal Conqueror pulled His sword from the vile composition and began to swim back to the surface. All of the other Fiends of Acheron and Sea-Snakes appeared to be wounded, from this innermost rupture; their various figures began to slow down and float lifelessly around Him. It was an enormous conquest.

The Sacred Hero's mind was once again on His warriors above the surface. Had they listened to His commands? Had they fought as one army?

Above the surface, an apocalyptic array of fire and

mayhem was swirling around and the ground was still shaking from the underwater explosion, which had only just erupted. The anaconda-like serpents had given birth to hundreds of venomous lizard-like creatures called Basilisk, which were feverishly roaming around, emitting a lethal-gaze from their green eyes. The newly absolved army-of-heaven was fighting bravely, but nearly besieged under the measureless assault from the air and the sea. It looked as though many of them had been fatefully wounded, barely able to persevere and rise above the fierce oppression.

Absalom was shouting orders across the fire to a physically unimpressive man of Greek descent. The man, although undersized, was an able and fearless warrior and had naturally grafted a small number of souls into a masterful-defensive-position. Absalom was shouting for the group to graft into his own and form an even stronger wall of defense.

The archers were boldly firing into the dense air of destruction, striking hundreds of winged devils as they fell from the blackness. But, each of them, along with the myriad spear-warriors, was beginning to lose hope. Where was the Christ? What was the cause of the explosion beneath the fiery river? Had He somehow fallen amidst the smoldering sea? Were they all going to suffer an even greater punishment because of their treachery?

The Greek warrior had managed to assimilate his group into Absalom's and now both of them were calling out orders for the remaining souls of light to join them in the middle of the burning river. All who possessed the strength began to carry the wounded and make their way onto the violent-waters. Each of them fought the temptation of despair.

"Where is He?!" one of the ax-bearers yelled to Absalom. "Can we alone fend off the fury of damnation?"

Absalom raised his voice with supernatural resolve: "Remember what He spoke, '*Do not give in to fear, even if you cannot see Me!*' We must continue believing! We must not lose heart, no matter the darkness! We must fight as one! One heart, one mind, one spirit; with one resounding voice-of-faith!"

The light around them began to grow as each warrior received the emboldening words of David's son. "Hell shall not consume us, this hour, if we are clothed in the light of the Christ!!!"

The onslaught increased from the air as the Soldiers of Paradise lifted their shields in desperate protection. "Pray!!!" Absalom yelled, "Pray!!!" The multitude broke forth into an aria of mystical tongues of worship and supplication.

In that very moment, the Hero of Heaven rushed to the summit of the sea and broke the surface! As soon as He emerged, every saline-eye was upon Him. His wearied host of combatants felt the pangs of hope stir within them in full force, utterly entranced by their Otherworldly Savior.

The Hordes of Hell were driven to madness by the sight of the Holy One and began to unhinge, flying in deranged and disturbed patterns. The leviathans, basilisks and sea-beasts all began to lose their strength and will, just as they had, under the smoldering-waters.

Glimmering amidst the darkness, Jesus Christ spoke to the agents of Hell: "You shall not prevail! You shall not steal what belongs to the Ancient of Days! You shall not pillage the souls of My children!" He turned to His nascent army, "Stay on your knees, beloved warriors!" He turned back to the echoing halls of the seventh-level of Hades, "I declare the wretched Tiamat of Acheron Dead for all Eternity!"

The shadowy devils and fiends of the seventh-realm shrieked and aggressively began to retreat into the corners and caverns of Perdition. Within a matter of moments, the chaos was temporarily halted.

The Truth of God addressed His kneeling troops: "Rise, valiant souls." They all rose, in a triumphant daze. Many of their faded-bodies were bleeding and maimed. He began to call them to Him, one by one, and heal their wounds, speaking blessings of courage and strength over them.

After this mysterious display of power, He warned them not to grow careless, for although the darkness had retreated upon this sphere, they were sure to mount an even stronger attack, the lower they journeyed.

The small Greek warrior humbly stepped forward and courageously asked his Leader why they were descending into the lowest realms of Hell, when they were trying to escape damnation.

The Christ would not give a complete answer, for He coveted their trust and faith. And so, He replied: "If you continue to follow Me, you shall indeed escape damnation and even enter the very Gates of Paradise. But you must *follow* Me, against your own wisdom and understanding, against your own instincts and desires—this is what you did not do in your earthly-lives and it led you each into destruction. All of you entered the Underworld as rational self-reliant men and women in your own eyes; but you shall only escape it, as little children. Do not doubt Me, for I am your only way out."

And with these words the Hallowed King of Thunder turned His gaze, toward the southeast passageway, about two hundred yards in the distance and lifted His sacred-sword in the air: "Warriors of Mercy, we continue our descent!!!"

V

Upon the Earthly-Fallen-Realm the Virgin was weeping, along with her spiritual children: the followers of her Crucified Son. They wept in bitter sorrow and mourned with little solace. A sword had pierced her heart and she felt as if she were dreaming. Her Son's blood was dry but still visible upon her clothes. It was the Day of Rest, but her soul had not tasted anything but sleepless hours of grief.

    Her son John was consoling her with the Psalms of David, and all around the house, only silence and weeping could be heard. Each of the aching mortals present was unaware of the Eternal Battle that was taking place in the Heart of the Earth. They could not see past the horror of what they had witnessed on the hill, just outside of Jerusalem. They could not even visit the Messiah's Tomb, until the following day.

    Despair was all they could hear within, and without—ashen clouds had encircled their temporal sky. The Mother of God softly cried:

"O Light of mine eyes, my sweetest Child, how art Thou hidden now in the sepulcher?[iii] *I am rent with grief, and my heart with woe is crushed and broken, for I saw them slay Thee with doom unjust. Light more dear than seeing, O my Son most precious, how in a grave dost hide Thee?"*[iv]

Within the Virgin-Temple-of-God, the voice of her Crucified-Son spoke; rising from the Underworld like holy-incense:

"Mourn not for Me, Mother, as thou beholdest Me in the grave; for I thy Son, who thou didst conceive in thy womb without seed, shall rise and shall be glorified. And being God, I will ceaselessly exalt and ennoble those who in faith and longing magnify thee."[v]

John, the Apocalyptic-Poet, ceased from reading the ancient Psalms of David and observed his mother, trembling in the corner of the room, whispering through her tears:

"My eternal Son, I escaped suffering at Thy strange birth and was supernaturally blessed. And now, beholding Thee, O my Son, dead and breathless, I am pierced with the spear of bitter sorrow. But arise Thou, that I may be magnified by Thee. Arise now!"[vi]

The Apostle gently approached the Theotokos, but could not hear the voice of Christ within her heart: the heart, which was pierced by the Sword of Golgotha, as the aged prophet Simeon foretold. Silently, the Vanquisher of Hell spoke again:

"The earth, O My Mother, hath hidden Me by Mine own will. And the gate-keepers of Hades trembled at beholding Me clothed with a robe spattered with revenge; for I, being God, have vanquished Mine enemies with the Cross, and I will rise again to magnify thee."[vii]

The Beloved-Disciple placed his hand upon the Ark of God, seeking to comfort her, whose name means, *bitter*. The divine heat from the Virgin surged through his body like a flame; and he remembered the fate of Uzzah, who died having touched what was holy. But, her flame was like the Burning Bush that mystically appeared to Moses in the wilderness: ablaze with the presence of God, yet being not consumed.

John held his gaze in awe: from this bitter-daughter-of-Abraham comes forth the sweetness of Eternal Salvation for the race of men. This is what he was told; this is what he had seen and what he believed—but the sight of

Christ's death on the Cross, overwhelmed his heart. With trembling voice, the Evangelist whispered, "Mother, will our tears ever cease?"

The Virgin looked up and answered, "I grew up in the Temple of the Most High. Angels gave me food to eat. I heard their songs in my sleep and saw their eyes flash like lightning. They brought to me the silence of prayer, the joy of heaven and the peculiar news of God's salvation. I was not a stranger to them. But I have never seen their countenance so perplexed and astonished: *The angelic choirs are filled with wonder, beholding Him who rests in the bosom of the Father laid in the tomb as one dead, though He is immortal. The ranks of angels surround Him, and with the dead in hell they glorify Him as Creator and Lord.*[viii] A war is raging in the heart of the earth, John. We must continue to pray through our tears. Blessed are those who mourn, for they shall be comforted. Blessed are those who weep for they shall laugh."

The Apostle fell to his knees, weeping, clutching her hand. Below them the Invasion of Hell raged on:

As the Valiant Army of Redemption traveled down into the eighth-level of the Underworld, the Christ of Mercy was chanting under his breath, *"Mourn not for Me Mother, mourn not for Me."* This realm was overflowing with bridges and overpasses, which spanned all the way from one end to the other, connecting in complex patterns. There was no visible land below these overpasses—only blackness. They would have to make their way strategically from one bridge to the next in order to find the entrance to the ninth-sphere.

The soldiers were more fortified in spirit, having defeated the great Tiamat in the legendary River of Acheron. They were still in the midst of metamorphosis, but many were appearing slightly more solid and human than before, while others remained quite faded in form.

They were ghosts, possessing a wounded imagination and a timeless yearning for the Resurrection of the whole-man: the Trinitarian union of body, soul and spirit.

No one knew what to expect; at any moment the whole fury of Hell could rain down upon them once again. In this precise instant however, it was hauntingly silent—the eerie calm, which one feels before a storm.

They advanced behind the Light of Heaven, over an enormous Pallid Arching Bridge, which rested above the abysmal-territory. Some of the bridges were ashen and lifeless, while others were black with smoldering lava breaking through their cracks. The elaborate and convoluted structure held the imagination of an immeasurable spider-web and although there was nothing visible below them, there was a nucleus, which held the strands together.

The Pallid Arching Bridge held the Paradisal-armed-forces underfoot. There were shrouds of bridges above and below them.

The Monarch of Heaven turned to face His threadbare host-of-souls and released His most virtuous voice over the darkened sphere: "Stay your weapons of war; they are worthless here. The spirits you shall encounter in this realm suffer no affliction from seraphic-spears, blessed-bows, sacred-swords or angelic-axes. They are Spirits of the Mind and Demons of the Will—and even more toxic than the battlement-fiends you have encountered thus far. Choose your course within you and bind yourself to the will of Almighty God. It is for freedom that you have been set free, beloved! But, you must choose the Wisdom-Faith, if you are to persevere, for there is no true-deliverance apart from the love of virtue. You have not yet ascended to the Father, nor have I—but unlike Me, there remains within your vessels the remnant poison of iniquity and self-veneration. You are still-faded and vulnerable to darkness."

Every redeemed eye was upon Him as He persisted, "I, the Everlasting Word of God made flesh in time, declare to you in this Dungeon of Desolation that your heart and your tongue are the furthermost armaments of this realm. Resist the darkness, become the children of light that you are, and

the corruption of Hell shall flee from you! Above all, invoke My Name with firm reliance on the Grace of Heaven and the Sovereignty of God! We must prevail beyond this realm, beloved!"

Obediently, they placed their weapons of war in their sheaths and holsters, and felt the burning conflict of faith rise within them. It was wholly counterintuitive, but there was no option other than rebellion, and that would most assuredly mean defeat.

The Prophet of Armageddon turned around and continued over the colorless Arching Bridge, lighting the path by the sheer radiance of His glory and charisma. His countenance was transcendent, adorned with an unchanging resolve and determination. His robe shimmered in the darkness as He walked before the beloved of God, interceding for each of them. The fragile and diminished denizens of the Divine-Wake stepped cautiously forward, scorning the dread.

Suddenly, the bridge began to tremble beneath them; lightly at first, but the tremors increased rapidly. Immediate trepidation was felt within the rushing streams of the vulnerable-mass. No adversary could be seen, but the structure continued to shake. It was quaking violently now, almost to the point of rupture. Before anything else could be done, the Arching Bridge began to fragment underfoot, striking terror into the hearts of the renegade infantry, who were holding onto the serrated-sides and falling to the ground, desperately trying to hold on.

The Patriarch of Wisdom stood back and allowed the bridge to sever into pieces. Each division of the overpass was still connected to another part of the whole, but strangely moving, independent of the original arch. The army-of-light was being separated. Several souls fell through the widening cracks, hanging on to the edges with their bare hands, screaming. Their feet dangled over infinite darkness as the sections of the bridge swayed left and right, up and down. Others knelt down to save them and after more than a few moments of alarm; all were retrieved and lifted to safety—for the fleeting present.

The Shepherd of Deliverance stepped back onto a linking partition, which laid only a few feet behind Him and observed the vivid peril. No one else was able to reach the region where He stood—there was to be another trial of faith for the Sons and Daughters of Emancipation. He watched without passivity or acedia. He was not a stoic in His short earthly life, nor was He in the spirit-world-of-decay.

Some of His warrior-kin were crying out in abject confusion and fright, for the tentacles of the multifaceted configuration were moving with intelligence, and verve.

One of the women, a petite figure of Egyptian descent with salient blue eyes, named Theresa, attempted to raise her voice above the whirling-commotion: "Brothers and sisters of mercy, cling to one another and hold on to your emerging faith…" before she could finish, the woman was abruptly thrown onto her back with great force, along with many other suspended souls on her section of the severed-bridge. The atmosphere was revolving and spinning around, spawning a vertigo-motif.

Suddenly, swarms of fly-like creatures blew in and frenzied around the various fragmented partitions. A violent droning sound of bedlam overtook their ears. It was blaring and nearly intolerable. Most of the bridge-inhabitants covered their ears with their hands and knelt on the ground, hoping the incessant noise would disappear, but some lashed out in panic; striking the air with their weapons to no avail.

There were nine broken peninsula-like extensions, floating amidst a sea-of-darkness, covered by gloomy clouds of devilish-scorpion-flies. The pilgrim-warriors were still emitting light beneath the horde, but their opposition was only beginning.

Rising out of the swarming-din was a multitude of

unholy voices, whispering and converging in accusation. The shadow-priests-of-hell were murmuring and hissing the vilest stanzas they could envisage, pouring forth a multilingual chorus-of-condemnation. The fiendish voices were filled with the utmost rancor for every rebellious soul and it seemed as though darkness were overtaking both sound and sight. The feeble mumblings and ardent prayers of the beloved Image-bearers were muted below the horrid orchestration.

The Scapegoat of Humanity looked on, with a heart full of zeal and Élan. He was untouched by the cloud of scorpion flies and the demonic cascade of temptation, which covered His army-of-souls, no longer benighted. He had made His way to the center of the eighth-realm, where He could remain visible to all Nine-Fragments of the Shattered Arch. His spirit ached for His beleaguered army, but He held His restraint with incomprehensible sagacity.

Underneath the tattered feet of the temporal bridge-dwellers, the fiery-ashen substance of the overpass morphed into a reflecting pool. The faded-souls-of-amnesty felt the changing substance beneath them and turned their gaze toward the liquefied ground.

All began to behold a nightmare-vision of their own mirrored-image. They saw themselves out of the Eyes of

Evil; the most corrupted state of their abominable existence. Every soul was struck with horror, for none of them had beheld their own likeness, while living in Hades—the only memory they possessed was of their earthen dispositions; and although they had witnessed the faded dispositions of one another, these images were unlike anything they had conceived, until this dreaded-hour. The shock of these phantom-reflections plagued the hope of the redeemed and threatened the heart of their ultimate triumph.

The shadow-voices of Hell lifted their pitch and increased their fury, magnifying the demoralizing vision. The Wraiths of Gehenna relished the open onslaught of lies and violence of the soul.

Amidst the wearying clash of spirits, the Manna of Heaven broke His silence: "Children of Radiance, Descendants of Beauty, do not gaze upon these maimed and deviant images, but fix your eyes upon the Lamb of God! I AM your True Image! I AM the Mirror of your Future! I AM your Destiny! I AM the Truth of your existence! Look unto Me, and the shadows of this dominion shall never destroy you!"

Many began to lift their heads and turn their gaze towards the Sun of Righteousness, but others continued to be transfixed by their own image. The Only-Begotten of the Father spoke above the swirling blast of condemnation,

"As the wilderness-prophet Moses lifted up the image of a serpent and the Venom of Death could not pierce the wandering children of Israel, so long as they gazed upon it—so you, if you look unto *Me*, shall be shielded from the poison of this realm! Do not look upon the depraved reflections beneath you! Look unto Me! Look unto Me! I AM the firstborn of all creation! I AM the Image of Salvation!"

As He spoke, His eyes were like azure-flames of passion. The swarming clouds were moving erratically, as if His voice were a painful intrusion, releasing waves of interference into the atmosphere. The few warriors who continued to gaze upon their own image were suddenly sucked into the reflecting-pools by an unseen force, disappearing from sight. The shadow-priests continued to prophesy their abhorrent plots, but the dawning-faith of the Refugee-Pilgrims who persisted in staring at the Christ, was breaking the power of evil.

The voices persisted for an allotted portion of time, but the eyes of the redeemed were transfixed on the Lion of the Tribe of Judah. The Christ raised both arms high in the air and the great Arching Bridge began to tremble once again and supernaturally reallocate; grafting into itself, over the abyss. The clouds of scorpion flies withdrew into obscurity, the voices of the eighth-realm vanished and the demonic reflecting pool morphed back into its original pallid soil.

Their hearts were pounding, their minds were racing and many ceased to blink, as they slowly began to perceive the incredible occurrence, which had just manifested.

Delilah, the woman Christ had delivered from four demons, fell on her knees and began to worship Him. Others followed suit, bowing reverently, igniting their surroundings with the warfare-of-praise. This was an affair the Enemy of God could never have envisioned, except perhaps, in the deepest alcove of his subconscious fears: his slaves, worshipping the Son of God in the pit of Hell, suspended over his Chasm of Darkness.

Behind the splendid silence and over the meditative adoration of the Blessed One, the reverberating sounds of subterranean booms and thundering-roars began to rise to comprehension. The Commander of Avalon turned His head in recognition of the echoing resonance rumbling behind the walls and below the abyss of the eighth-realm. His fire-blue eyes shone amid the Absent-Light.

The River of Light moved swiftly over the complex maze of bridges; swerving from one appendage to the next. They made their way down from one tentacle to another as one-body-of-faith and luminosity. At every turn they sensed a greater strength rising within them, even though they were approaching the most feared realm of Damnation.

The winding-descent seemed to go on ad infinitum and there was no entrance to the lower-sphere. The haunting reverberations behind the barrier-walls only magnified as they climbed down the myriad burning overpasses. What could be waiting for them on the other side? The Ruler of Hell had not been seen since he vanished into the recess of a dusky cave, ages ago. What could the Father of Evil be preparing, underneath the shadows of the eighth-region?

Suddenly, thousands of feet below them, hanging over the void in the middle of the abyss, the faintest glow of fire could be seen. It could very well take hours for them to reach it, they thought, but it seemed as though the mind of every soldier who saw it, came to the same awareness: this small, glimmering flame was the Burning Entrance of the Ninth-Level-of-Hell.

VI

The doors barring the entrance to the Ninth-Region possessed a deep and foul knowledge of evil. The inferno, which covered the ominous doors, burned with malice and wild perversion. The spirit-warriors were clearly fatigued from fighting against godless-hymns of anxiety and woe. They were about to enter the abdomen of the Abode of the Dead.

The Resplendent Carpenter approached the large, narrow doors and whispered something in an unknown tongue. They began to rumble, as if the dynamism of His voice had caused some unseen force to rupture them. The noise began to blend with the thunderous reverberations, coming from the other side of the surrounding walls.

The army of heaven-bound-ghosts readied their mystical weapons. They had witnessed the wrath of Hell as prisoners, and also fought against the winged-minions of the upper-realms and the sea-beasts of Acheron; but nothing could prepare the imagination for what was on the other side of these doors. This would be the last stand—and they knew it.

The Veritas-Illuminata touched the blazing entrance, pushing the doors wide open. A blistering wind rushed over them as they walked in, suffused with adrenaline. But, to their utter astonishment, the Sweltering-Hall was silent and bare. The strident sounds they had been hearing for the past several hours were unexpectedly gone. The large, narrow doors closed behind them as the last of the light-militia bounded in.

They were a considerable remnant of fleeing-souls. But they felt rather diminutive in the vastness of the Sweltering-Hall. Everyone manifested the cadence of his or her own uniqueness; some comforting and extolling those nearest to them, others retreating into the solitude of their own thoughts. A few souls were desperately cowering within, but it was a minority, for the presence of the Master-General was crushing to the fallen-nature of those who believed.

In the distance, lay the jagged blasphemous-altar, which held the vision of the Christ, during His cosmic-execution. This same, Christ of Eternity, made His way along the soil of the cursed-temple, towards the altar in the middle of the hall: "Keep your eyes open, faithful ones..." He said, without turning around; "...silence does not mean solitude; the darkness of this realm never sleeps."

He wanted to show His warrior-saints the altar where He had undergone the Ultimate Sacrifice. He wanted them to see the place where God's mercy and justice had triumphed over sin and death. But, this was not the only reason He had battled so heroically, leading them all the way to the Belly of Sheol. This was not the reason they were traveling through the Ninth-Level of hopelessness.

That was yet to be revealed.

His robe was glowing in the night-cavern as they reached the altar. The Beloved Son leaned over and touched the altar with both hands; the heavenly-throng watched His every move. It was not unlike His posture in the mournful-garden of Gethsemane. His disciple-ghosts knew nothing of these earth-heroic details, beyond what He had proclaimed to them in the beginning of His incursion. But they sensed the magnitude of it, in the bosom of their spirits.

Absalom could also perceive a deep sorrow emanating from the Divine Son. He approached his Lord, "Master… only a few have fallen away."

"Each one is the world to Me. There was nothing I could do." Jesus Christ looked up with tears in His eyes, "Don't you understand? I am helpless before your freedom."

Absalom looked at Him, utterly overwhelmed by the

love he felt in the Messiah's eyes. The Suffering Servant raised His head slowly and turned around to face the remnant-army: "Upon this altar, the Son of Man took upon Himself, in spirit and in truth, the sin of the world. Each one of you, precious and invaluable souls, have been preserved from damnation. Shame is no longer your god. Fear is no longer your master. Has darkness been able to steal even one of you from Me? Have not all of your pneuma-wounds been healed by the touch of My hand or the words of My mouth? No one could have opened the jaws of your fiery prisons, if I had not suffered, both upon a Roman Cross and upon this Altar-of-Hell. All of the myriad persuasions and transient-philosophies of your solid-life find their fulfillment in Me. I am the *Master Carpenter* of the Asiatic-Prophets and the Cross of Golgotha is the eternal *Sword of Compassion* your ancestors spoke of. I am the True *Avatara* of the Hindu-Aspirations, who descended from the Heart of Heaven to enlighten a blind world! I am the True *Balder* of the Norse-Yearnings, for in My death I have brought about the destruction of the gods! I am the True *Osiris* of the Egyptian-Mythos, the *Lord of Love and Silence,* and *God of the Afterlife;* by Whose imminent Resurrection, all may attain eternal life with the One Veritable Ruler of Heaven. I am the True *Ahura Mazda*, of the Zoroastrian

dream: the uncreated God and upholder of *Asha*! A star
shone in the heavens and led their priests to the stable-temple of My birth with gifts of gold, frankincense and myrrh
as offerings of their worship and devotion! They prostrated
their bodies in humble reverence and whispered holy-awe
in their Avestan tongue; proclaiming through visionary
deed how every pagan-soul is summoned to bow before
the Only Son of God! I am the realization of the Syrian
Shadow, *Hadad-Rimmon*; whose lamentations were but a
faint silhouette of the cosmic mourning of Calvary! I am the
True *Lord of the Earth,* like the shadow-god of fabled-legend,
who died and rose again in ancient myths and lore—I have
fulfilled these sagas and mended the scattered pieces of
the Divine Mosaic. No longer shall your darkened-souls
look upon the Infinite Mystery as a ruthless, mercurial,
bloodthirsty god; but a loving Father of Mercy and Light!
The One-True-God never demanded or desired the blood
of your children for absolution! You have always remained
the beloved sons and daughters of heaven's unchanging
affection. Even in your most wretched, barbaric state of
confusion! It was not yours, or your children's blood that
was desired for your redemption, but *My* Blood! The uncontaminated Blood of the Spotless-Lamb! No longer shall
you fear the unrighteous anger of an impulsive-god or the

haunting nightmares of a shifting-deity. It is God Who has died to rescue you; the Word-of-God-made-flesh! It is My Blood that offers mercy, protection and favor! It is My death that gives you life, not your own! I AM the *Prophet* that the Hebrew deliverer Moses spoke of! I AM the *Fire* and the *Voice* of the Burning Bush! My Body and My Blood are the *New Covenant*, of which Jeremiah prophesied! I AM the *Logos* behind all Revelation, of which Plato and the eminent Greek philosophers sought knowledge! I AM the Way, the Truth and the Life! The Beginning and the End! I complete myth and fulfill legend—I transcend all shadows and shades of fragmented Reality! My Name is written in the dust-filled, bloodstained history of man: I entered time as the factual, unfeigned Salvation of God! I died on a Roman Cross under the reign of Pontius Pilate; not in the wandering mind's eye of a soothsayer or the wishful dreams of an unsound-oracle—but *within* your history of flesh and blood! I AM the Consummation of all Desire and the only Complete-Revelation of God! This is My message to you, redeemable-spirits-of-mercy! I AM the Love and Grace of Almighty God; the Hope of Man!"

    Holy silence hung over the desolate air of Ancient-Rebellion. His face shone brighter than ever before. His eyes were cosmic and flashing. He was unrivaled in beauty and magnificence. It was almost as if the Sweltering-Hall of Hades had been transformed into Heaven itself, by His mere presence. The army-of-souls had momentarily forgotten the raging war in which they were engaged; they were lost in the magnitude of His passion and purity.

Flames shifted along the cavernous walls, disturbing the reverent silence. He sensed the coming-war and moved swiftly toward the dismal southern-shadows. No one knew what He was doing or where He was headed. He turned around just before entering the dark-threshold and faced His warrior-children.

He instructed them to keep watch over the flames and silhouettes, citing their expansion as telltale signs of an impending attack. He also admonished them to remain in the hall and not to follow Him, but to fearlessly lift their hearts up to Heaven. He could easily discern the muted-trepidation, which lived below each mask-of-valor, so He plunged His Empyrean-Sword into the sable ground beneath Him, releasing a protective womb-of-light around the godly-assembly. The Soul of Civilization seemed intent on a wholly different concern than His acolyte-ghosts. He crossed the dark-threshold of the southern-shadows and mysteriously vanished from sight.

Having watched their Hero disappear into the blackness,

the Zion-Destined men and women swallowed their apprehension, as best they could. He had done this before, they thought, at the River of Acheron and had returned. This, along with the shield-of-light, allayed much of their fear, but not all of it. Where was He going? Would this womb-of-light really protect them, until His return? The Children-of-Exodus began to gather, drawing strength from each other's presence. Some bowed their heads, some knelt on the ground, others lifted their eyes at the surrounding-light with awe—but all of them entered into the mighty battle-craft of prayer.

Inside the darkness, the God of Angels advanced, voyaging through a subterranean serpentine-passageway. There were no flames to proffer illumination in this forsaken-tunnel; He alone was its Source of Light. There were no prisons or chambers possessing the souls of the dead—only an endless and barren path.

He thought of the Halls of Paradise and the illustrious Banquet awaiting Him and His Rescued-Beloved. He thought of the echoing compositions His angels would construct in honor of the Blessed Ceremony. He saw the New Jerusalem in His mind's eye—the Tree of Life and the glistening Celestial River, calmly flowing through His Father's Kingdom. He envisioned the revolving skies, undying beauty and wondrous creatures of the highest Realm of Serenity.

He thought of His earth-bereaving disciples: Peter, the Sons of Thunder, and each of His fragile apostles, one by one. He pictured His Mother's face; her beautiful, innocent and comforting smile. He heard the laughter of fellowship and the colliding discourse of holy alliance. These thoughts strengthened His hallowed resolve.

And then, after untold depths of darkness, He abruptly stopped, something had suddenly appeared from the shadows: before Him stood the bars of a lost-ancient-prison. There were no flames viciously decorating this chamber of Hell; only cold, abandoned stones of bitter sorrow and regret. He could not see the inhabitants of this dungeon, but He knew their names and the reason He had come.

He walked through the stone-bars and into the epic-dungeon. Even the great-darkness of this place was as light to the Eternal-Seer-of-the-Ages. He called out to the shadows; the same heroic-voice that restored lepers and raised the dead to life:

"Man of Dust and Spirit, First Born of Grace and Truth, Guardian of Eden, Patriarch of the Fallen, son of God fashioned from the Womb of the Earth, Prototype of the Blessed Image... *Where are you?*"

The Author of Atonement raised His undefeated arm,

shedding a piercing ray of light, revealing the Original Man. He was crumpled and distorted: a shadow-vapor. His appearance was unnaturally aged, as if he had continued to disintegrate, without the rest-of-death. Time was an eternity here, but also a blink. The man had been in this vacant-cave since the curse-of-time had caught his heel, and yet, he had only just arrived.

He recoiled violently at the Blinding Light, which stood before him—for his state of darkness could not bear the Presence of Perfection. The Guardian of Eden writhed in pain and torment, the weight of unspeakable shame pressing upon his spirit, like an ocean of remorse.

The Enemy of Love had kept the Fabled-Man here, in the lowest-realm of condemnation, as the crown of his Sadistic-Invasion; the hidden and Tormented-Monument of his Eden-Raid and glorious revenge on the Ruler of Heaven. But one invasion deserves another, and the Almighty was unyieldingly determined to have the final word:

"Arise, Man of Sorrow, and open your eyes!" The decrepit-figure struggled to his feet, unable to lift the veils, which covered the windows of his immortal soul. He feebly stood up, his hands shielding his face from the searing brilliance of the Christ. The broken-vessel trembled with fear and wept, as the Word of God spoke with eternal compassion: "I am not here to torment you, beloved Adam, but to save you. Remove your hands and show Me your eyes."

The shuddering-figure slowly removed his hands and opened his blackened-eyes. Immediately, they flashed white and his sight was consumed. His eyes were open, but all he beheld was blazing light. His voice quivered: "Who are you?"

"I am your Offspring; and I have *'bruised the head of the Serpent'* as was prophesied on the Day of Destruction. My Spirit walked with you in the Garden, and clothed you in your nakedness after you kissed sin. I have come, at the End of the Age, to the suffering-pearl-of-great-value and ransomed your children from the sting of death. I have fulfilled the cosmic-covenant-of-perfect-faith, which you and your wife betrayed. I was crucified once, for all men! The sins of humanity are forgiven! For if, because of one man's trespass, death reigned through that one man, much more shall those who *receive* the abundance of grace and the free gift of righteousness reign in life, and the afterlife, through the one man Jesus Christ, who stands before you now. On a Roman tree-of-violence, which by the power and majesty of Almighty God was transformed into the redemptive Tree of the Knowledge of Good and Evil, the sins of the world were atoned for! This Roman Tree-of-Judgment-and-Mercy is the Flaming Sword that turned every way, guarding your entry back into Eden. The governorship, which had been given to you from the beginning by the grace of God, and abdicated through your faithless-iniquity has been recovered and given back to Me, the *Second-Adam*. The Prince of Darkness no longer possesses authority over the souls of your children, Adam. I have taken authority, rule and jurisdiction back from the Father of Lies; the earth is once again My footstool by right, for I have swallowed up the sins of man and My reign of righteousness shall never end. I am here to set you free and give you the gift of eternal life!"

The decaying-ghost was no longer weeping. He was standing erect with broad-white eyes, staring into the misty haze of his dreamlike vision. The Christ of Paradise walked over to the blind-patriarch and reached out His holy hands, touching Adam's eyes, mercifully. His vision flooded back into him, like an ocean of wonderment filling both iris and pupil. As the waters of ecstasy rushed through his blood, the Ruler of Heaven prophesied over His first-born: "Behold the Image of your True-Self."

As these words caught the desolate wind and blew over the spirit of Adam, his withered appearance began to transmute from a loathsome and cursed-specter to a youthful heroic-spirit of promise. His sight and form were shifting beneath a windstorm of revelation. The curse of death was unraveling around him, like a winding-burial-cloth, which covers the departed.

When the whirlwind subsided, Adam gazed upon the Nazarene; He was stunned and overwhelmed to the core of his spirit. The Image of Christ roused a burning memory of his own mysterious reflection in the streams of Eden—but it was infinitely more glorious and radiant. The Fallen-Child fell to his knees and worshiped the Son of the Most High with silent tears of rejoicing. He was in a euphoric-state of unimaginable thanksgiving. He could not move or rise to his feet by his own strength, nor could he speak; he was being baptized in the sea of agonizing-bliss.

He had seen the vivacious colors of the earth suddenly fade away; he had witnessed the sky above him darken in judgment, he had felt the terrifying awareness of shame and nakedness penetrate the pores of his skin and the heart of his soul. He had beheld the heavenly splendor of his wife wither and die before him; he had heard the cry of his murdered son, echo over the fallen-valley. He had observed the unrestrained wickedness of his own mind and the weakness of his injured-will. He had lived long enough on the cursed-earth to see the evil of his myriad offspring abound.

He had witnessed all of these ominous-clouds-of-decay,

as the only-soul who could have prevented their gathering-descent. And now, in the Belly of Hell, he beheld the One-Soul, who could overturn and reverse all of the chaos and darkness he had ushered into the world—the Light of Men, the Grace of Heaven, the Christ of Regeneration.

Adam looked up, rose to his feet and gazed upon the Mirror of his True-Humanity, in utter awe. A measureless-moment passed between them.

Then, from the deep tormented shadows of perdition, the unchaste Mother of All Living emerged, adorned in fear and infamy. Like her mythical-husband only stations before, she too was pitiful and distorted, but the Author of Re-creation could perceive the shining-innocent-child, buried beneath her demonic veil. Her face was cold and wonder-struck. The sight of the Heavenly-Messenger was vast enough for her darkened senses, but it was the transformation of Adam that gripped her with dread. She suddenly felt alone, like she had in those fateful moments between her original transgression and her husband's acquiescence.

In the Fabled-Garden, she had stood naked before her husband as a sudden-mortal, while he stared at her from a distance, with a sinless gaze. He was still the innocent and undefiled man of God, but she was now contaminated and

doomed in some unknowable way. The conversion in the Garden was not physical at the outset, but an inner inexpressible-ache, an intangible mourning, which was utterly foreign to both of them.

Adam had walked over to his radiant-beloved in soul-shock and curious dread. He did not know if what he was sensing in his bowels was real or a dream, for the un-fallen did roam in the realm of dreams. Nothing had changed in her appearance. Had God lied? Why the dire warning; and that strange word, *death*? What did it mean? The one discernment of which Adam was somehow desperately clear was that whatever this change meant, he would forever be apart from Eve, unless he joined her.

A fearful rush of rebellious adrenaline gripped his imagination. The choice between God and the flesh of his flesh and bone of his bones was cosmically before him. He knew Whom he should trust, but he took the mystical-fruit and shed the blood of his own innocence. It was then that the sky darkened and they felt the winds-of-shame blow over their skin.

Eve felt the vital-pangs of this memory flood through her like lightning-blood. She looked back at the Anointed One and her corroded face trembled with ancient emotion. Adam reached out his hand and spoke to the woman: "Eve, behold the Holy Offspring who was foretold to us in our Hour of Grief; He has accomplished our atonement. He has done, what I failed to do; bruised the head of the serpent and dethroned the Dragon of Perdition. He has undone the works of the Devil and usurped his dreadful-dominance by becoming the Human-Lamb-of-God: an everlasting sacrifice, wholly pleasing to the Almighty. He has overthrown the Father of Hell; and He offers us free-emancipation from the chains of torment. He is the Song of Salvation, Eve!"

The transient-woman knew not where to place her eyes, for she longed to gaze upon the glory of her Deliverer, but a mantle-of-shame weighed heavy upon her spirit. Echoing in the chambers of her mind was the profusion-of-curses the Serpent had spoken over her, after the sky had darkened:

"No longer are you the Mother of all Living; but you are now the Mother of the Dead, a womb of misery and a temple of shame. You have made yourself a god of ruin and devastation. No one will ever redeem you, Eve. You are an abomination and your name will fall off the tongues of your dying-children, like a song of mourning and lamentation. Your blood shall cover the whole earth and the bones of your babies shall return to dust. This is what it means to be a god."

The Christ could hear the echoing-curses flowing through her mind and silenced them, with the flame of His tongue:

"Daughter of Eden, Crown of Creation, Beloved Eve; hear the voice of your Hidden-Hope, look upon the Face of your concealed-desire, step into the light of your wounded-longing. I have taken your guilt and washed your iniquities with Sacred-Blood." The cadence of His voice began to unshackle her spirit, as she fixed her feeble-eyes upon Him. "I am the First-Born of all Recreation. All died with Me on the Tree and all who believe in Me shall rise on the last day to everlasting life. I am here to free the captives of Hell by the purity of mystifying grace; for I am headed back to the Middle-Sphere through bodily resurrection and then to the right hand of My Father-on-High. Will you journey with Me, Daughter of Grace, back to the gates of Paradise? Will you receive the gift of heaven? Take My hand, beautiful one, step into the Aching-Light of forgiveness, rebirth and metamorphosis. Don't fear the light, little one; it shall only consume the darkness, not you."

The ghostly-woman stared at the spirit of the Galilean, overcome with emotion. Without further vacillation, she rushed into His embrace and disappeared in the Light. Adam observed in holy reverence, mystified by the unfolding vision.

When the woman emerged from the globe-of-light,
she had been transfigured into a youthful spirit-of-hope
and eternal-destiny. She looked at the image of Adam and
could tell by his expression that she too had been reborn.
The Warrior-Christ looked at them with joyful urgency:
"Blessed Children, you must follow Me, for The War of the
Underworld is upon us!"

And with these words He swiftly departed, with the
redeemed-patriarchs-of-humanity in His wake.

VII

By the time Heaven's Offspring emerged from the southern shadows with Eden's Progenitors in His train, the floor of Hell was already shaking violently. Scorching debris was descending from the swirling sky, striking the shield-of-light, which covered the spirit-warriors. His sheep immediately felt His presence and were infused with liberation at the sight of Him. The three sojourners entered the womb-of-light, evading the falling fragments of fire, which had transformed the Sweltering-Hall into an apocalyptic-landscape.

Upon entering the light-shield, the Commander of Angels spoke: "Our flight to heaven begins, now. We must ascend to the highest region of the Underworld to escape the malefic abyss. This is the portion of the penitent-ghosts of Hell; the destiny of God's exonerated-children. Each of you, men and women alike, great and small, were fated for this campaign, born for this conflict and awakened for this warfare. You are all covered in the Armor-of-God; your hearts, shielded by celestial-mail, your hopes, protected by sovereign streams-of-grace and your spirits, sheltered by the Father's love. Take My yoke upon you in this hour and learn from Me! I am the Creator of eternal-warfare—Author of the art-of-holy-battle. Faith, hope and love are the highest weapons of battle-craft. Keep your peace, beloved. Remain watchful and alert! Know, Whom it is, that you serve and fear no evil, for I am with you! These minions of darkness rely on fear and deception to defeat My flock; but it is they, who have cause to fear, for the Son of Almighty God rides before you this hour! The vengeance of heaven is upon Me, and the pure-flame-of-love shall not be overcome! Fight for the sake of love, for the songs of your children and the memory of your future! Give your heart to the neighboring-spirit who fights beside you, your soul-friend and saintly-companion. When your spirit is wounded or besieged, cry out to the Spirit of Resurrection! Fight in the power of My Name, under the authority of heaven, by the Blood of My Cross!"

    He looked around, giving His eyes to as many of His warrior-children as He could. The hellish-comets were still raining down upon the protective-shield: "You're the most beautiful mass-of-sinners I've ever seen!" The army erupted with joy at His well-timed humor. He lifted His eyes at the seemingly endless voyage before them, then looked back and firmly spoke: "In truth, you are now lights in the darkness; Image-Bearers of the Uncreated-Trinity. This is the appointed-hour, to avenge your brutal enslavement! When I leave this womb-of-light, it shall disappear from above you; and you must fight in the Spirit of God, if you are to survive. Fear not, little flock, for the battle is already won!"

    Again, the crowd rejoiced and lifted their weapons triumphantly in the air. The ground was still shaking as the Head of Heaven stepped out into the fiery chaos. The womb-of-light vanished, as He said it would, and the army-of-saints lifted their shields, in defense. A deluge of demonic-forces frantically descended, augmenting the maelstrom: winged-devils, flying-serpents and shadow-fiends, all raining down from various locations of mayhem. Beasts of Hell broke through the walls on every side, along with countless slithering-ophidians pursuing Christ's children with speed and malevolence.

    The King of Battle led His courageous convoy quickly through the beastly-barrage, slaying droves of them with the might of His blade. The sacred-warriors instinctively maneuvered their fated-weapons with the grace of angels and the ferocity of savages; holy vengeance was pumping wildly through their blood. They made it past the abominable-altar, all the way to the entrance of the Ninth-Realm; but the immense doors had vanished.

The way out was not the way in.

The Deliverer turned without delay and peered into the never-ending darkness of the western-gorge. Through the smoldering wreckage, He perceived an upward tilt in the ground: their only escape was to battle through the entire forces of evil and ascend to the Middle-Sphere, where they would encounter the resurrection-dawn.

He raised His ageless-sword and charged headlong into the wrath of Hell. His soldiers followed Him, consumed with heavenly-madness and immortal-insanity. Archers released mystical-arrows, which divided in mid-air, striking the falling-ungodly spirits around them; spear-warriors drove their lances deep into the gruesome land-fiends, along with the ax-bearers and swordsmen, impaling the ghostly-horde with their blades. The apprehension, which had plagued some at the River of Acheron was gone; replaced by an otherworldly confidence and fearlessness. They took ground swiftly, with the Wind-of-the-Spirit at their backs.

The ground had shifted imperceptibly from a level plane to an ascending slope. They were pressing upward, into an unknown division of the Underworld. The pathway began to narrow but the onslaught persisted. The Prince of Peace smote every demonic-force in His path, with the thrust of His righteous-blade and the radiant beams-of-light, which emanated from the wounds on His hands. He ordered the light-bearers to close off the entryway, which they had just passed through. The Children of Paradise battled valiantly with the gleaming-weapons of faith and virtue, acquiring noble-wounds, where the fangs of diabolical fear and doubt had penetrated beyond their armor. It was uncertain whether the narrowing-path would work to their advantage or not, but they continued to fight as if it would. A fragment of the spirit-warriors banded together, pushing great jagged-stones, at last, closing the entrance.

It grew darker once more, as they made their way into the neck of the cave. The falling-comets had temporarily subsided, but the remnant-ambush continued to haunt them. The distant-sight of the western-entrance of the Sweltering-Hall began to diminish; but there was no approaching-light that could be seen in front of them. All souls seemed to know instinctively that the jagged-stones could only hold the ravenous-fiends at bay for so long.

They progressed deeper into the vast tunnel and soon, the glow of the Carpenter was the only source of light around them; along with the crimson-eyes of the remaining serpentine-devils, who were deviously seeking to puncture the spirits of the chosen ones. The Children of Grace continued to slay them, wherever they emerged and soon the wretched-tunnel grew ominously silent. The valiant-army once again became a River of Light, voyaging closely together in the wake of their Master. The passageway was long, but an undercurrent of anticipation was swelling within the hearts and minds of the new-heirs of the kingdom.

   Darkness followed darkness upon each advancing-step and then suddenly, without any manifest-cause, the Christ of War began to hasten into a full-charge. As soon as this occurred, the ground began to quake underfoot, breaking apart in several places, like severing ice. The multitude began to shout aloud, apprehending what was taking place in their midst. They began to charge forward, in imitation of their Shepherd-King. The ground began to give way behind them, crumbling at their feet, revealing an inferno, hundreds of stations below. The last of the throng ran with all of their faith and might, barely escaping their doom with each stride. Just as it seemed the inferno would swallow them whole, the Light of the Universe lowered His shoulders and burst through an unseen-wall-of-darkness, into a wide-open realm of Hell.

The River of Light landed in a vast-plane, narrowly escaping the wrath of the haunted-tunnel.

Peace, however, was not to be found in this new-region of Perdition. The heavenly-host gathered itself as quickly as possible, still reeling from the near-defeat. They looked around in awe at the Mines-of-Mourning. Transient-Altars of human sacrifice were strewn about the sweeping-enclave. The presence of sorrow hung like a dense fog over the demented atmosphere. The echoing-sounds of children, infants and innumerable wrath-god-appeasers, resounded throughout the bloodthirsty region, chronicling in chaos the disturbed history of God's orphaned children.

The Reconciler began to place His hands on the transient-altars, ending the cries of each one. He looked at His army of cleansed-souls and spoke: "Go and do likewise, for you are all one with Me now."

There was little hesitation, but much amazement in the eyes of His ghostly-children. They spread out like the brilliant-wings of some heavenly griffin, and began to heal the memories of each altar. They climbed the crevices of the Mines-of-Mourning and anointed the stones-of-sorrow with the Solace of the Everlasting Christ. Each spirit-physician naturally gravitated toward the echoes of their earthly-mother-tongue, for nearly every tribe and language since the dawn of death was swirling in their midst. One by one the tormented-cries began to abate, as the spirit-apostles glided throughout the region, in hallowed-harmony.

Tears fell from the face of Jesus, as He absorbed the sacred-healing, so gloriously occurring through His Presence and Power.

He released an impassioned soliloquy into the urgent atmosphere:

"These blood rites; these pagan-shadows, are the dreams and nightmares of children without a Father, the anguished-adolescence of humanity; for they possessed fervency without knowledge, superstition without faith, impulse without wisdom, fear without revelation and guilt without the consolation of the True-Atonement. These are the songs of orphans: the Grace-Seekers and Benighted-Heirs to the Kingdom of Heaven. Now is the hour of your burning-consummation, the descending-light of your soul's supplication and the undying-salve of your mending-dispensation and solace: there is only One-Sacrifice acceptable to God, and He has accomplished it Himself, through the blood-baptism of His Son."

Once more, the ground began to tremble with rage. Rumblings of war were felt above, below and around them. The stones-of-sorrow began to fall rapidly, dismantling the altars and fusing into the wasteland. Sounds-of-approach could be heard, coming from the haunted-tunnel they had only just emerged from. "Make haste!" the Light of Heaven spoke, as He began to move quickly beyond the visible-plane, into the shadows again.

But the shadows only revealed a greater darkness.

Appearing out of the depths of misery was a spirit so colossal it caused the fleet-of-heaven to draw back, dazed by the sight. The creature was swiftly rising hundreds of feet into the air and began to spread its colossal-wings across the entire Armageddon-sky. The last portion of the massive-beast to unfold itself was its towering-neck and terrifying-countenance.

Flames were glowing within the chambers of its mouth and steam rose from its nostrils. Every eye now perceived with dread: the blood-curdling-creature was the Dragon of Perdition—Lucifer, in all his wretched-might! The Keys of Hades still hung around its neck.

The soldiers-of-welkin cowered in intuitive defense, but Jesus Christ stood upright and beautifully-calm. He stared at the ancient villain fearlessly; threatening him with the weight of His sinless-eyes. The Dragon reared its neck back and to the side, seething with unrestrained wrath.

The myriad fiends-of-hell transcended the walls-of-the-mine and surrounded the remnant-sojourners, who moved promptly into the sheltering-shadow of their Shepherd-King. The vile-spirits were too awestruck by the manifestation of their Towering-Ruler to pursue the fleeing-souls further.

Every spirit present; from the foulest devil, to the most human ghost, watched the immortal-clash unfolding before them, in fearful- amazement.

The Dragon was writhing in torment and anguish, summoning his original-madness, which sought to dethrone the Most High. The Word of God had witnessed the ravishing-angel fall like lightning from heaven; and He stood before his diabolical-rage once more, in the spirit-form of a man. The Christ was small in stature, standing before the enormous Dragon, but He was magnificently unflinching and fiercely radiant. In His azure-eyes, lived the very power, which created the heavens and the earth. The hope of every soul was burning within His breast and His spirit was aflame with triumph. He continued to stare at the Dragon, unafraid by the ostentatious war-spasm of the Prince of Darkness.

The Dragon reared back violently as the Warrior's gaze echoed victoriously throughout the realm. The Incarnate-God held out His arms, signaling His troops to brace themselves.

    The demonic-throng began to chant and clash their weapons; stomping on the ground in lustful-unison. They had seen their Dread-Sovereign destroy the Messiah before, on the Cross, numinously arrayed on the blasphemous-altar of the Ninth-Realm; what was to keep him from doing it again? The frenetic-chanting rose to a fever pitch and the great Dragon inhaled his bottomless-wrath with all of his might and released a whirlwind of blazing-fire upon the Hero of Heaven.

    The fierce and relentless vortex blew over the Shimmering-Christ like a tempest-of-fury, but He was unmoved, completely able to absorb the ancient-indignation. His hair and robe were flowing gracefully within the barrage of bedlam.

    The onslaught seemed endless as the Dragon continued to emit the fullness of his ire. The blaze washed over the Christ and around the River of Souls behind Him, leaving the sons and daughters of paradise unharmed.

    In the midst of the whirlwind, the Radiant One lifted His ageless-sword high into the scorching-air and spoke:

    "Accursed Spirit of Damnation! Author of Rebellion and Deceit! Dragon of Perdition! The flames of your wrath are as the wind to Me! I have no foiled-veins for the venom of your anger and contempt to infiltrate! Shall you consume the Maker of Fire? Shall the heat of your envy devour the One who spoke from the Burning Bush? You cannot prevent My ascension; nor those who follow and cling to Me— you cannot imprison the Son of Righteousness! You cannot vanquish the Holy One of Israel! I have suffered death for the life of the world; and I am rising again as the first-born of all creation. The Kingdom of Heaven is at hand! The Kingdom of Light and Virtue, the Reign of Love and Mercy, the Rule of Grace and Truth, the Dominion of Peace and Justice, the Kingdom of Joy and Reconciliation! I will wipe away, every tear from the eyes of My beloved children, and you shall *never* wound them again. It is finished; Light has overpowered Darkness, and Love has overthrown the Father of Lies! Dragon of Hell... your reign has *ended!*"

The Hero of Heaven flung His sword forcefully at the breast of the Dragon. The flashing-sword flew effortlessly through the firestorm and struck the age-old Serpent of Rebellion! Upon impact, the firestorm ceased, the Keys-of-Hades fell to the ground and the Dragon began to thrash about, wildly in torment. The assembly of devils watched in horror as their Master plummeted to the ground, shaking the very foundation of the Underworld.

The Dragon flailed about on the broken-floor in wounded agony. The army-of-pilgrims rose to their feet, injected with holy-triumph.

How could they be stopped now?

"*Follow Me!*" The Lion of Judah exclaimed, as He retrieved the burning Keys of Anguish, leading the charge into the unknown-realm, which lay before them. The fugitive-children rushed past the wounded Dragon in shock, utterly speechless at the sight of Hell's Ruler, who was astonishingly unable to halt their escape.

The suffused mass-of-warriors disappeared into the shadows. The Dragon began to convulse and shift-his-appearance back into the Fallen-Angel-Lucifer. Two of his most fierce generals recovered from their demoralized-trance and hurried to his side. They assisted him to his feet and reached for the Sword-of-Christ, but it was too resplendent for them to grasp. The Devil pushed them away in injured-pride and tried to regain his balance. His breathing was labored and his strength was faint. He whispered under his breath: "My reign shall never end; my reign shall never end." He turned to his distressed-minions, indignant and summoned all the authority he retained, "Am I not still your Ruler? Have I not defied the Most High and pillaged the storehouses of heaven? Have I not murdered and raped the fate of His wretched-children? Are my chambers not filled with the tormented cries of His disavowed-beloved? What are you all staring at? Are they not my slaves? Are they not still within my borders? Pursue them to the end! Show no mercy! Bring me the soul of a weakling to feast on and regain my strength! Go! Go now!!!"

The Host of Hell pressed into the ascending-shadows in pursuit of the remnant-army.

The armada-of-saints had rapidly wound their way from the adjacent Mines-of-Mourning back to the seventh-realm, where the River of Acheron lay, sleeping. The region was quite different from when they had first descended upon it, under a deluge of assault. The river was indeed confined, and the walls-of-fire were flickering feebly; unable to intimidate the ghosts-of-clemency. They ascended without a trace of confrontation or fear. Only the faint-curses of those spirits who had chosen the illusion-of-darkness over the Revelation of God could be heard.

The resplendent Bridegroom-of-Humanity led His beloved higher, into the sixth-level of anguish, where the Feasting Hall was arrayed. It too was barren and posed no threat to the advancement of the refugees.

The flashing–multitude passed the numerous prisons like a tidal wave of dazzling-light. They rushed through the remaining regions of Hades like an electrical storm.

They transcended the fifth, the fourth and the third level of the Underworld with increasing momentum and emergent-strength. Each spirit was rapidly transforming: their eyes, their form and their countenance were all becoming more visibly-solid and they could feel the coming restitution in the bosom of their souls.

They passed the second-level of destruction and washed ashore on the very tier where the Christ had made His illustrious-proclamation over the entire assembly of the Absent-Light. He led them back into the same cave He had emerged from at the onset of the Invasion.

Once again, darkness fell upon the children-of-morning as they traversed into the shadowy-halls. The gleaming-brilliance of the Overseer was the only star in their war-torn-night to guide them. They voyaged through the dense-shadows, higher and higher. It all seemed like an unending dream, which they prayed they would never awake from. They possessed the pressing-anticipation of un-born-infants within their souls; they were all womb-dwellers, awaiting the imminent conversion of the elements.

Tears of hope streamed down the faces of many, for the first time since their earthly-youth.

Suddenly, the Icon of God slowed to a halt. The faintest sound could be heard, beyond the walls, surrounding Him.

His eyes flashed like a tiger hunting his prey. The Christ of Mercy tilted His head ever so slightly, following the sound to His left. The sacred-verse, which the Immortal Poet had etched into the cursed-wall at the beginning of His incursion, became visible: *I have led captivity captive.* His Blood trembled within as He reached out His immaculate hand and touched the coarse-wall, sensing the nearly inaudible vibrations streaming through. He stared at the jagged rocks, as if looking into the abyss of eternity. A strange remembrance came over the Everlasting Warrior: when the Uncreated Light touched the walls of the Virgin's womb and felt the presence of the Glorious Forerunner so near. Were they once again silently calling one another, blood of blood, from beyond these darkened walls? Could it be? The Voice of One Crying? The Candle of the Light? The Knight of the King?

Suddenly, out of the dense shadows a frail voice whispered, "Master! I have been waiting for You!" The Seeker-of-the–Lost turned his gaze toward the shadows as the figure of an old man slowly emerged. The man was of Chinese descent, dressed in a dirty white robe. The back of his hair was long and pulled tight behind his head; his thin, grey beard streamed down over his chest like a waterfall. His eyes were both ancient and young. The Sage limped his way closer and fell to his knees, overcome with emotion, staring at the ground:

"I have waited for You; You Who have no form; no beginning and no end. The One who fills all things by emptying Himself. The Way has appeared to me, Your unprofitable servant, and I am undone! My words are corrupt and vain! Now that my eyes have beheld the face of the Uncreated Sun, I am blind! Behold Master… I am blind!" The Ancient Sage began to weep, for he was seeing visions of the crucifixion.

The Christ knelt down with haste to raise the old man to his feet, "My friend, my dear *Lao Tzu* rise to your feet! You are not blind; your eyes are being healed." A white film rested over the Sage's eyes. The Beautiful Physician touched the man's eyes, restoring his sight. As the white film faded, the Light spoke, "You have come to show Me the way to the Assembly of the Righteous!"

The Ancient Sage stood in awe, transfixed by the sound of the Warrior's voice and the countenance of His face. The army-of-saints stood behind the Christ, shimmering like stars as the Seer spoke: "How can I show You the way, Master? *You* are the Way—the Unknowing. How could I show You anything You do not already know?"

The God-Man smiled at His servant, "Nevertheless, it

is fitting for you to lead Me to the Forerunner. His voice is crying out to Me!"

The Ancient Seer erected himself and with the innocence of a child, he obeyed. Lao Tzu gingerly limped over and faced the dark wall. He raised his right arm and began moving his hand over the surface of the wall, back and forth, up and down, mystically burning ancient Chinese symbols upon it. As he did this, the Sage whispered into the darkness of Hades:

"Hell was filled with bitterness when it met Thee, O Word, for it saw a mortal deified, marked by wounds yet all-powerful; and it shrank back in the terror at this sight. Hell was wounded in the heart when it received Him whose side was pierced by the spear; consumed by divine fire it groaned aloud at our salvation who sing: O God our Deliverer, blessed art Thou."[ix]

As the sacred-markings blazed in the darkness, a door began to materialize: the same mystical-door, which Christ had not been permitted to enter at the dawn of His descent. "This is the way, Master," the Sage said, meekly.

The *Pantocrator* stepped forward, burrowing His eyes into the serrated-barrier and proceeded to walk through the door. The Ancient Sage followed the Light, as he always did in his earthly life. The multitude poured through the burning door in waves-of-light.

Upon entering the other side, the Warrior of Wisdom gazed upon the Assembly of The Righteous, with the Locust-Eater standing in the midst of them. This same John, who was the first to proclaim the Christ upon the outer-earth, stared across the lifeless-hollow at his Lord and King. Murmurings within the Sacred-Assembly slowly abated, as the Ruler's presence was made known to all. The dark-hall was barren and vast; it seemed to be untouched by the forces of evil, set-apart and hidden from the Great Dragon.

The Master-Ascetic held a torch in his hand and spoke with the voice of a god: "Behold, the Lamb of God, Who takes away the sins of the world!" The hallowed-multitude erupted in thunderous shouts as Jesus Christ approached them, with the fire-of-heaven flowing at His feet. Weeping could be heard as the souls of the righteous witnessed the Son of Man in the realm of the dead. Men and women of every race and tribe swarmed around Him: Hebrew prophets and righteous kings, pagan sages and philosophers: men and women of earthly-renown and nameless-saints known only to the One Who inexplicably stood before them now. They appeared more like gods than mortals: Abel, Noah,

Melchizedek, Abraham, Isaac and Jacob, Joseph, Joshua and Caleb, David and his Mighty Men, Solomon and Sirach, The Queen of the South, Tobit, Tobias, Esther, Samuel, Judith, Hannah, Jonathan, Deborah, Isaiah, Elisha, Jeremiah, Ezekiel, Daniel, Malachi, Heraclitus of Ephesus, Pythagoras of Samos, Socrates and Plato, the eminent disciples of Lao Tzu, a myriad of Sibyls and priests: blacksmiths, widows and orphans, carpenters, artists and scientists; the poor and the rich, young and old, all who gave their lives in complete-surrender to the Light they were shown during the temporal-age. It was a sea of faces, outnumbering the stars in the sky.

    The Christ of Love walked amidst the assembly, which stood in *Abraham's Bosom*, taking in each beautiful-face, as if it were a sacred-dream. The time had come for the holy to be released from Hades. He made His way through the crowd to the Forerunner with tears in His eyes, falling upon his neck.

    "Master!" the desert-dweller exclaimed.

    "The time has come to raise the dead, John! My Father has sent Me to save the very dregs-of-hell, for He is not willing that any should perish!" With these words the Word-of-God turned and addressed the sacred-assembly:

    "Beloved souls of the Kingdom of Heaven! The Most High has heard your prayers! The Son of God has delivered the Patriarch from the depths of Hell and destroyed the power of death!" The assembly released another roar, shaking the very walls of Sheol, "Behold your ancestor, ADAM!!! Behold his wife, EVE!!!" The ground trembled beneath their feet, barely able to hold the heavenly-bound-host: "We must leave at once; upon the earthly-realm the dawn of the third-day is approaching! Follow the Light and move as one! Do not be afraid! The gates of Heaven are within reach!"

 The Chieftain of Praise led His holy-legion out of *Abraham's Bosom* and back into the winding halls-of-perdition. They persisted along the ascending-darkness, feeling the change of elevation in the marrow of their resurrecting-bodies. Their senses were flooding back to them in all their original-purity. They could perceive the atmosphere-of-life returning to their lungs. They traversed with blinding-speed, higher and higher, as if the wretched-realm had no end.

 The Christ of Refuge rounded the final dim-corner and halted before an unassuming-wall. The glow of His Presence lit the surrounding area enough for many to see. But there was no way out to behold, only a jagged wall of earthen-rock. Many of the pilgrims looked behind them, sensing the pursuit of Satan's army. The Forerunner could feel the presence of fear entering many of the refugees. He turned back, peering into the vast darkness.

The Savior reached out and touched the wall with His pierced-hand and a circle-of-light began to burn into the cave. The wall shook deeply and crumbled around the circle-of-light, opening a door to another world—but the opening was barred by a large gate made of brass with iron bars. The Conqueror of Hell lifted the keys, which He had taken from the Dragon and held them in the air, "Behold, Children of Light! He Who holds the Keys of Death and Hades!" The Master of Deliverance placed one of the keys into the lock and spoke in an unknown tongue.

Suddenly, a blinding-light burst into the cavern, virtually knocking the flock-of-souls to their knees. They covered their eyes, avoiding the searing pain of re-birth. The Gates of Perdition lay broken and shattered beneath the Savior's feet. The sound of thunder arose within the Halls of Hell. No one could perceive what direction it was coming from, nor could they see anything, for the light had blinded their eyes. The Son of God raised His voice above the roaring sound, "Hold on to one another!!! Do not be afraid! This water is for your eternal salvation!!!" Suddenly, a raging river burst through the doorway into the cave, washing over the multitude, knocking them off their feet. The water was violent and cold. The Army of Light was scarcely able to withstand the force of the waves. As the children of heaven emerged from the water, taking deep breaths, their faces became radiant, like the sun. But, they could still not see.

The Deliverer stepped onto the threshold as the Bridge between the two spheres; His eyes burned with sacred fire, as the waters of Jordan rushed below Him. He turned back and addressed them urgently:

"Children of Heaven, you must act quickly! Do not withdraw from the light of your redemption. Your eyes will only be blinded for a short time. When you cross the threshold, and begin the next stage of your journey, rest assured; you shall not be alone. Each of you shall have a *messenger* to accompany you and to guide you. You shall recover your sacred-sight along the way and take hold of your eternal-resurrection. Stay with your guide and you shall reach the Gates of the Third-Heaven!"

Many began to open their eyes in spite of the pain and saw to their astonishment, multitudes of heavenly-spirits descending towards the opening; gathering behind the Christ. The King of Glory took Adam by the hand and delivered him to Michael the Archangel; Eve quickly followed, clutching her husband's hand back into Paradise. The Immortal Son charged Michael forcefully, "Take them and their children home at once!" The resplendent Archangel took the Patriarchs and vanished into the blinding light. Celestial-beings rained down as far as the eye could see and Absalom, who was still among the first-line of warriors, watched in dreamlike wonderment.

The Elysian-Commander called one of His angelic-servants to Him and began to release His orders, "Titus-Gabriel, assist this valued-soul to the gates of My Father!" Jesus reached out for Absalom's hand and led him across the blinding-threshold. Absalom took the hand of his angel and proceeded into the mesmerizing-landscape of resurrection, void of natural sight.

The Majestic-Messiah summoned the following messengers to His side, "Ariel and Raphael! Kemeul, Ramiel and Valoel! Lion-hearts and Saints-of-Grace: Caleb-the-faithful, Elisa-the-fair, Adora-the-innocent, and all messengers-of-war; assist the sons and daughters of triumph to their rightful abode in the Everlasting Kingdom!"

He ushered His remnant-sheep swiftly through the mysterious-opening and into the sea-road-of-paradise. Each soul was entering the blinding-realm with willing-trust and surrender. The River of Light was flooding into the resurrection-dawn!

The Forerunner once again faced the darkness of Hell and cried out with a Song of Deliverance. His voice was thunderous and torn from all his years, crying out in the wilderness. Rescued-Souls rushed by him towards their redemption. The water, with which he baptized the Christ in the River Jordan, flowed beneath him. His voice echoed, filling the Realm of the Dead:

Today hell groans and cries aloud: 'It had been better for me, had I not accepted Mary's Son, for He has come to me and destroyed my power; He has shattered the gates of brass, and as God He has raised up the souls that once I held!'

Today hell groans aloud: 'My power has been destroyed. I accepted a mortal man as one of the dead; yet I cannot keep Him prisoner, and with Him I shall lose all those over whom I ruled. I held in my power the dead from all the ages, but see, He is raising them all!'

Today hell groans and cries aloud: 'My dominion has been swallowed up; the Shepherd has been crucified and He has raised Adam. I am deprived of those whom I once ruled; in my strength I devoured them, but now I have cast them forth. He Who was crucified has emptied the tombs; the power of death has no more strength!!!'[x]

More and more souls rushed through in utter-bliss. Every tribe, race, tongue and nation were bursting through the opening, into the luminous-realm-of-salvation. The entire assembly was chanting with one voice, shaking the very foundations of Hell, *"Christ is risen from the dead, trampling down death by death and upon those in the tombs bestowing life!"*[xi]

The River flowed gloriously into the serenity of forgiveness and eternal-destiny. The fiends-of-damnation were haunting the darkness with their approach as the remaining souls poured over the threshold, into their ultimate-escape. Christ the Lord attended His ear to the coming-horde and quickened the pace of the exodus. The mass-of-souls were almost entirely through. The sounds of pandemonium grew violently near, as the last remaining fugitives crossed over into the realm-of-angels. The Forerunner took one last look at the Christ of God and walked into the light.

As the Good Shepherd raised His hand to close the portal, a frail and young and beautiful-spirit turned back and spoke to Him with illumined-eyes, "But where are You going? Are You not coming with us, Lord?"

He lowered His gaze at His beloved daughter, "Soon, child. I must return to the Middle-Sphere and proclaim the mystery of the Resurrection to the dying. I will be with you soon, do not fear little one; I am always with you. Now go, quickly!"

The child-of-heaven departed and the Judge of the Living and the Dead raised His hand once more to mend the shattered-wall. The portal closed miraculously just as the demonic-horde rounded the corner of the cavern and stopped dead in their tracks at the sight of the Son of God.

He turned to face them in all His fearsome-radiance:

"When I come again, it will be the end of you. Depart from Me, spirits-of-hell!" He raised His defiant-arm and violently thrust a raging-shaft-of-light across the air, knocking them back into the blasphemous-shadows. A small avalanche-of-stones crumbled to the ground, barring the passageway.

The Savior was alone in the throat-of-the-Underworld.

He looked a short distance to His right and saw the artless-thoroughfare back to the earth. His spirit-form had nearly finished reconstructing itself into a solid-body.

He slowly walked the short distance to the narrow entryway, which led upward like a flight of stairs. The eternal weight of this moment rested upon His mind like a mystical-shawl. He climbed the jagged stairway and pressed into the ceiling-of-mire above Him with His sacred-hands.

He crawled back into the tomb-of-judgment—into the

history-of-man and closed the earth beneath Him.

It was pitch black and silent; and in the darkness, the Light of the World knelt down upon His knees and praised His Heavenly Father. Hours passed by within seconds as the Son of Paradise lifted His heart, soul, mind and strength upward, in unbridled love and affection for His Father; burning with anticipation for His Homeland.

Suddenly, Celestial-Light broke upon the cave like the first-sunrise of Creation, welcoming the Morning Star of Resurrection. The sepulcher could not hold the Poet-of-Immortality, Who mysteriously walked out of the sealed-tomb.

The New-Song-of-Salvation peered out upon the mystical-earth. The ground beneath His feet began to violently tremble and the heavy Stone-of-Death began to roll away from the entrance of the tomb.

Having swallowed death once for all; Jesus Christ stepped forth into the epoch of an Everlasting-Dawn!

EPILOGUE

But on the first day of the week, at early dawn, they went to the tomb, taking the spices they had prepared. And they found the stone rolled away from the tomb, but when they went in they did not find the body of the Lord Jesus. While they were perplexed about this, behold, two men stood by them in dazzling apparel. And as they were frightened and bowed their faces to the ground, the men said to them, "Why do you seek the living among the dead? He is not here, but has risen. Remember how he told you, while he was still in Galilee, that the Son of Man must be delivered into the hands of sinful men and be crucified and on the third day rise." And they remembered his words.

Luke 24:1–8

O blest, blest world!
Thy God hast not forgotten thee,
Whence His Son descended so,
Thy darkness broke into a million pieces,
Of vanquished perjury.

Into thy helpless night,
Cometh thy saving Light,
To light the world's dim sight,
With Grace's flashing-might!

THE BEGINNING

Death could not devour our Lord unless He possessed a body, neither could hell swallow Him up unless He bore our flesh; and so, He came in search of a chariot in which to ride to the underworld. This chariot was the body which He received from the Virgin; in it He invaded Death's fortress, broke open its strong-room and scattered all its treasure.

Saint Ephraim the Syrian

i   C.S. Lewis, *Myth Became Fact*, an essay published in *God in the Dock: Essays on Theology and Ethics,* (First edition, Eerdmans, United Kingdom, 1970 original copyright by the Trustees of the Estate of C.S. Lewis) cslewis.com under the section, "The Centrality of the Christian Story".

ii *The Gospel of Nicodemus,* this exchange is a paraphrase of the dialogue between Hades and Satan, translated by M.R. James, (Oxford: Clarendon Press, 1924) scanned and edited by Joshua Williams, Northwest Nazarene College, earlychristianwritings.com

iii *The Lenten Triodion*, translated from the original Greek by Mother Mary and Archimandrite Kallistos Ware, First published in 1978 by Faber and Faber Limited, 3 Queen Square London WC1 Printed in Great Britain by Western Printing Services Ltd Bristol (Reprinted with permission 2002 by St. Tikhon's Seminary Press South Canaan, Pennsylvania 18459) p. 643

iv *The Services of Great and Holy Week And Pascha*, According to the Use of the Self-Ruled Antiochian Orthodox Christian Archdiocese of North America. Arranged and Edited by V. Rev. Father Joseph Rahal. (Anatakya Press, Englewood New Jersey, 07631-5238), pp. 563, 569

v Ibid. p. 558

vi Ibid. p. 558

vii Ibid. p. 558

viii *The Lenten Triodion*, translated from the original Greek by Mother Mary and Archimandrite Kallistos Ware, First published in 1978 by Faber and Faber Limited, 3 Queen Square London WC1 Printed in Great Britain by Western Printing Services Ltd Bristol (Reprinted with permission 2002 by St. Tikhon's Seminary Press South Canaan, Pennsylvania 18459) p. 646

ix Ibid pp. 648, 650

x Ibid pp. 655, 656

xi The Paschal Troparion

About the Author

Jonathan Jackson is a multi-dimensional artist: a poet, actor, musician, and filmmaker. His previous works include a book of poetry entitled, *Book of Solace and Madness* and the theological prose, *The Mystery of Art*, which has since been translated into Greek, Romanian and Russian.

Jonathan's life in the arts began as an actor at the age of eleven, where his performances garnered him five EMMY Awards. After many years working in feature films, he starred in the renowned television drama, *Nashville*. As a musician, he is the lead singer and songwriter for the band Jonathan Jackson + Enation.

He was recently named Associate Dean and Primary Lecturer at Theoria College of Filmmaking in Houston, TX. Over the course of three decades, his journey as an artist and public speaker has taken him to many places around the world, including Ireland, Italy, Romania, Russia, Canada and Greece. He currently resides between Ireland and Tennessee with his wife Elisa and their three children. For more, visit www.JonathanJackson.com

Printed in Great Britain
by Amazon